MILLS AND INDUSTRY. This picture is of a small, quaint mill believed to have been located in Atkins. The first recorded gristmill in Smyth County, owned by Arthur Campbell, was built in 1777 on Staley's Creek. Water provided power to operate these first industries. (Courtesy Kenny Sturgill.)

IMAGES
of America

SMYTH COUNTY

IMAGES
of America

SMYTH COUNTY

Kimberly Barr Byrd and Debra J. Williams

ARCADIA
PUBLISHING

Published by Arcadia Publishing
Charleston, South Carolina

Library of Congress Catalog Card Number:

For all general information contact Arcadia Publishing at:
Telephone 843-853-2070
Fax 843-853-0044
E-mail sales@arcadiapublishing.com
For customer service and orders:
Toll-Free 1-888-313-2665

Visit us on the Internet at www.arcadiapublishing.com

RED BRICK COURTHOUSE. This courthouse was constructed in 1834, two years after the county was formed. The building was made of red brick and was used until 1905, when the present courthouse was built at the same location. (Courtesy Kenny Sturgill.)

CONTENTS

ACKNOWLEDGMENTS

Efforts have been made to verify the facts and dates included in this book, but in many instances different dates have been found for the same event. Neither the Historical Society of Washington County nor the Museum of the Middle Appalachians is responsible for the dates given or the contents of this book. This volume is not intended to be a formal or thorough history of Smyth County, but merely a visual tour of the many changes in Smyth County's development through the years.

High-quality prints of images supplied by the Museum of the Middle Appalachians in Saltville or the Historical Society of Washington County in Abingdon are available for purchase by contacting them in person. We encourage you to help preserve our rich heritage for future generations by allowing your local historical society to scan your old photos, letters, or other materials.

Please take a moment to look at the names of those who contributed photos for this book. We would like to express our sincere appreciation to everyone who provided materials. Without their generosity, this project would not have been possible.

We would like to express our sincere appreciation to the following people: Dean Adams, Cecil Barr, Phyllis T. Barr, Malcolm Brown III, Bill Calhoun, Jerry Catron, Rick Davidson, Linda T. Dean, Beverly Evans, Zollie Fowler, Annie Frances, Jim Glanville, Watson Gollehon, Patton Graham, Judge Charles Harrington, Bill Honaker, William "Bill" Lemmon, Danny Lowe, James McNeil, Roy McNeil, Ralph Millsaps, Elmer Phillippi, Lawrence Richardson, Carol Rosenbaum, Joe Sayers, Debbie Schwartz, Charles W. Seaver, Ed Sheets, Tom Totten, Richard Walker, Jimmy Warren, Mark Warren, Jeff Weaver, Joy Carol Williams, James Wood, the late Charles Wassum Jr., Shannon Williams, and Todd Yates.

A very special appreciation goes out to Harry Haynes and staff of the Museum of the Middle Appalachians in Saltville, who have gone well above and beyond the call of duty. Also, we would like to thank the staff of the Smyth Bland Regional Library and the Smyth County Chamber of Commerce.

This book is dedicated first and foremost to our Lord and Savior, Jesus Christ, who makes all things possible that would otherwise be impossible. Secondly, we dedicate this book to our husbands, Mark Byrd and Joey Williams, for their love, support, and encouragement.

So, catch a rainy day, grab a warm drink, find a cozy corner, and prepare to sit a spell as we reminisce of times gone by.

INTRODUCTION

In 1748, James Patton led a group of men to survey 120,000 acres of land granted to him by the king of England. Charles Campbell, Dr. Thomas Walker, and John Buchanan were part of this expedition. Charles Campbell claimed the Buffalo Lick Survey, and John Buchanan later settled in the Rich Valley area.

Smyth County, named after Gen. Alexander Smyth, who represented this area in Congress, was formed in 1832 from parts of Washington and Wythe Counties. The breathtaking mountains, wide river valleys, and rich natural resources have contributed greatly to Smyth County's development. The Holston River, which naturally directed the paths of those who settled here, divides the county into three valleys.

Nestled in the mountains of Southwest Virginia, Smyth County is rich in history. Many towns can trace their history back only a couple hundred years, but due to excavations, Saltville's history can be traced back more than 14,000 years. The most complete musk-ox skeleton ever found in North America—outside of Alaska—has traced Saltville's history back to the Ice Age. The earliest archaeological reference regarding the Smyth County area is from Thomas Jefferson's journal, his notes of a mastodon tooth from Saltville given to him by Arthur Campbell.

In 1750, Samuel Stalnaker built his home near present-day Chilhowie. Later, Town House was built as a fort and eventually expanded to become a stagecoach inn. Town House offered early frontiersmen protection against the Indians and later served as a meeting place for the soldiers of the Revolutionary War, War of 1812, and Civil War.

Industry played an important part in our early development. Mills, which were necessary for grinding wheat and grains as well as providing power, sprang up throughout the county. In 1770, Arthur Campbell built the first recorded mill in this area on Staley's Creek, the first west of New River. Soon, every community of any size with water frontage had a gristmill. In 1835, three years after its formation, Smyth County had 16 gristmills, 14 houses of worship, a cotton factory, 3 iron works, a courthouse, a jail, several mercantile stores, and 8 taverns.

Religion was very important to Smyth County's early settlers. The first church in this area was built in 1766 in the Royal Oak section—present-day Marion. It was constructed by Arthur and John Campbell at their sister's request and named Royal Oak Presbyterian Church. The camp meetings that began in 1818 at Sulphur Springs were the start of the Chilhowie Methodist Church

Smyth County has been home to several governors, delegates, senators, and Supreme Court justices. Many brave and famous leaders have resided here. Two of Virginia's governors—David Campbell and Henry C. Stuart—came from two of the county's first families. Campbell wrote of Smyth County's settlers, "The first settlers on Holston River were a remarkable race of people, for their intelligence, enterprise, and hardy adventure."

Smyth County was of great importance to the Confederacy during the Civil War because of the large salt deposits in Saltville, the nearby lead mines in southern Wythe County, and close proximity to the railroad. By 1862, Saltville provided most of the salt for the Confederacy. Salt was essential for food preservation, tanning hides, and human consumption. After marrying Elizabeth Henry Campbell, Gen. William Russell moved his new family to Buffalo Lick, later called Saltville, and began producing salt. In 1799, William King expanded production to begin the first commercial salt-making industry.

In the early 1800s, the Chatham Hill community was the location of a shipbuilding industry. These ships provided the quickest means of transporting goods prior to the railroad's arrival in 1856. Flat barges measuring from 60 to 90 feet in length and up to 16 feet wide were manufactured here and used to transport goods to the newly opened markets along the Ohio and Mississippi Rivers. These barges were floated down the North Holston to Kingsport and Knoxville, Tennessee, and occasionally as far as New Orleans.

The "Home Guard," a group of men either too young or too old to join the armed forces, defended Smyth County until December 1864. Gen. George Stoneman and his 4,000 troops penetrated the county, destroyed the railroad bridges and the Thomas Iron Works, and temporarily disabled the saltworks.

The brave citizens of Smyth County have supported their country in war, and some have paid the ultimate price: during World War I, 16 Smyth County citizens lost their lives, and 111 died during World War II. Korea claimed 15 of our young men, and 12 lives were lost in Vietnam. We salute those who have served and those who continue to serve their country so unselfishly.

In 1982, Smyth County celebrated its sesquicentennial. Although at times faced with its share of adversity, Smyth County continues to move forward. With new employment opportunities filtering into the area and the expansion of tourism, Smyth County is winning the battle, and the future looks very positive.

Thousands of years ago, God placed his hand upon an area of land in Virginia and decided that it would be one of the most beautiful places on the planet, alive with natural beauty. He created rolling hills, lush valleys, and tumbling creeks. One has only to visit a large city, return home, and gaze at the natural beauty that surrounds us to realize how God has truly blessed us.

JOHN MONTGOMERY PRESTON HOUSE. This is an early photo of "The Ford," which was built on the site of an earlier log tavern. John M. Preston built this handsome structure, hoping to change the bad reputation given to the area by the previous tavern. During the Civil War, Gen. George Stoneman and his Raiders took possession of the house, turning the first floor rooms into horse stalls. (Courtesy Kenny Sturgill.)

One

MARION AND
SURROUNDING COMMUNITIES

On February 23, 1832, Smyth County was formed from parts of Washington and Wythe Counties by an act of the General Assembly of Virginia. A committee was appointed to locate a site for the new seat of justice. Because of its central location within the county, Marion was chosen and was recognized as a town in 1835. The town was incorporated by the General Assembly on March 15, 1849. The early town of Marion consisted of approximately 27 acres purchased from William and John Hume's 280-acre tract. The town was named in honor of Gen. Francis Marion, a hero of the American Revolution. After the railroad was built in 1856, Marion began to grow rapidly. The railroad provided quick transportation of lumber, lead, manganese, and locally grown products to the market. Local businessman William H. "Bill" Jones developed Mountain Dew, Marion's most famous product. This legendary drink was sold to Pepsico in 1964. The town has been designated as the "Home of Mountain Dew." In 1995, Marion became an official Virginia Main Street Community. As the gateway to Hungry Mother State Park, it is endowed with an abundance of natural beauty.

BUSY, BUSY, BUSY. Note the multitude of diagonally parked vehicles in this busy downtown scene. (Courtesy Clegg Williams.)

COUNTY'S FIRST COURTHOUSE. On April 19, 1832, the county's first court proceedings were held in the home of John Thomas. The first circuit and superior courts were held here on April 30, 1832. The Thomas home was used for two years while the original courthouse was being constructed. Located behind the Marion Baptist Church, this home was built by John and Arthur Campbell in 1766. (Courtesy Kenny Sturgill.)

PRESENT COURTHOUSE. Built in 1905, this building once contained an auditorium on the second floor where many public events were held. This structure was remodeled in the 1970s, but, according to this photo, not much changed on the exterior. The Marion Baptist Church behind the courthouse was torn down in order make room for parking. (Courtesy Dr. Paul Brown.)

ROYAL OAK PRESBYTERIAN CHURCH. A log church constructed in 1776 was the first meetinghouse in the area. Margaret Campbell refused to relocate to this area until her brothers, John and Arthur, promised to build a church. Once they were established, they built the first church in the Royal Oak community near the Marion Primary School. This photo is of the third Royal Oak Presbyterian Church. (Courtesy Dr. Paul Brown.)

THE CHURCH QUEEN VICTORIA BUILT. James H. Gillmore, a prominent attorney, bought property on Main Street to build an Episcopal church. Mrs. Gillmore sought help from Queen Victoria of England, who also was Episcopalian. With the queen's financial aid, the church was built and services began. The church was torn down in the 1940s to make room for the Parks-Belk store. (Courtesy Kenny Sturgill.)

MARION COLLEGE. Founded in 1873 by the Lutheran Synod of Southwestern Virginia as Marion Female College, the college closed at the end of the school year in 1967. Students were offered standard subjects as well as modern languages, music, drawing, painting, and waxwork. The present building was constructed in 1912. Male students were not allowed admittance until 1933. Blue Ridge Job Corps is currently located here. (Courtesy Dr. Paul Brown.)

MARION MALE ACADEMY. This private school was built just after the Civil War. The first teacher was William E. Evans. D.C. Miller was the first principal, and he and his son, Phipps, taught here. A.T. Lincoln was one of the many prominent men who attended the academy. This school now serves as a private residence and is located at 343 College Street. (Courtesy Debra Williams.)

MARION'S OLDEST SCHOOL HOUSE. Built in 1838, this frame building once sat on the corner of Church and Strother Street. Additions were made in 1884 to convert it into a residence. Clara Hill Carner saved the structure from demolition and was instrumental in moving it near the stadium of the high school, where it served as the Smyth County Museum for many years. (Courtesy Kenny Sturgill.)

SITE OF UNION OFFICERS' HEADQUARTERS. After the Civil War, Confederate states were required to conform to military rule. To ensure this, Union soldiers were stationed in different communities. Three hundred soldiers occupied Marion, camping between the I.O.O.F. building and the James White Sheffey home. This home of Military Commissioner Capt. William O. Austin served as Union headquarters and was located just west of the Blue Ridge Job Corps. (Courtesy Debra Williams.)

RUTH
THE MOABITESS
—A—
DRAMATIC CANTATA

SEAVER ⊚ OPERA ⊚ HOUSE,

THURSDAY NIGHT, **JULY 11,**

8 O'CLOCK.

Personations:

Ruth	Miss Alice Pendleton
Naomi	Mrs. Geo. W. Richardson
Orpah	Miss Emma Sprinkle
Boaz	Mr. J. N. Luther
1st Jewish Maiden	Mrs. C. O. Lincoln
1st Reaper	Wm. C. Pendleton
Israelitish Woman	Miss Lula Carrier
1st Messenger	Mr. W. H. Adams
2nd "	Mr. H. R. Huddley
Assistant Reaper	Mr. J. S. Pendleton

Semi-Chorus of Reapers. Semi-Chorus of Binders.
Semi-Chorus of Gleaners. Full Chorus of Israelites.
Chorus of Male Voices. Georgeous Oriental Costumes.

General Admission, 25c. Reserved Seats, 50c.

RUTH THE MOABITESS. This program is for the play *Ruth the Moabitess*, which was shown at the Seaver Opera House, the current location of Tinder Box Antiques. Located on the second floor was a stage, which became the gathering place for public performances. General admission was 25¢, and reserved seats were 50¢. Notice that gorgeous oriental costumes are advertised as part of the play. (Courtesy Malcolm Brown.)

SEAVER OPERA HOUSE. W.C. Seaver came to Marion in 1844 and started Southwest Virginia's first furniture manufacturing company. In 1884, Seaver expanded his store on Main Street, which housed his furniture and undertaking business. Local legend says that this is one of the most haunted buildings in Smyth County. This was also the beginning of the Seaver-Brown Funeral Service. (Courtesy Kenny Sturgill.)

14

MARION THEATRE. Pictured is Marion's second theatre, an annex of the Hotel Marion located on Church Street. It was managed by Oscar "Rabbit" Stephenson, and music was played by Mrs. Jesse Blackwell. The first picture show was operated by Dolphus Hutton on the lower end of Main Street in the area of Morrell Music. Both were silent theatres. (Courtesy Kenny Sturgill.)

MAIN STREET C. 1950. One can gather from this photo that downtown Marion was a very busy place. Notice the marquee for the Center Building, which was advertising *Man from Colorado* at the Lincoln Theatre. The old parking meters have since been removed. Today, trees line attractive downtown Marion, where building fronts have been restored and historical granite monuments installed in the brick-lined sidewalks. (Courtesy Charlie Snider's family.)

SITE OF CENTER BUILDING. This old boarding house on the corner of Main and Broad was removed in the late 1940s to make room for the Center Building. Constructed by Charles C. Jr. and John D. Lincoln, the Center Building once housed a theatre on the second floor. A bowling alley was located on the lower level, and retail shops and offices were located throughout the building. (Courtesy Kenny Sturgill.)

MARION SKATING RINK. Ala Carte may be one of Marion's nicer restaurants, but before 1945, a skating rink was located at this site. Southern States Co-op and Grissom's Auto Parts later occupied this space. More recently, the Harwood Company was located here and at another site on Matson Drive. This clothing manufacturer employed hundreds of locals. (Courtesy Kimberly Byrd.)

SMYTH COUNTY CENTENNIAL CELEBRATION. Pictured here is the county's centennial celebration, which took place at the Smyth County Fairgrounds on May 27, 1932. A historical play written by Laura Scherer Copenhaver was presented by Marion Junior College, the county high schools, and local citizens. Miss Smyth County, Eleanor Fairman, spun the wheel of time and scenes from local history were acted out. (Courtesy Kenny Sturgill.)

SMYTH COUNTY FAIRGROUNDS C. 1916. Smyth County Fairgrounds had all the makings of a big city fair. There were carnivals, food judging, games, and races of all kinds. The bandstand doubled as bleachers for viewing the horse races, with the homestretch of the track located directly in front of the bleachers. The building in the center, pictured here, contained seating for judges. (Courtesy Dr. Paul Brown.)

DIP DOG STAND. Located along Highway 11 at Preston Hill, the Dip Dog Stand has been a favorite local fast-food restaurant for many years. Dip dogs, their specialty, are wieners wrapped in breading and covered in mustard. They are also famous for milkshakes and ice-cream desserts. Recently, this drive-in restaurant won several awards, including the awards for best cheeseburger and for best service. (Courtesy Spunk and Pam Hall.)

TROLLEY CAR RESTAURANT. The structure in the middle of this picture, located on the corner of Main and Commerce, was once the Trolley Car Restaurant. At least part of this eatery was the Marion and Rye Valley Passenger Car #29, which later became the Twin Diner shown here. Another train car was used as the Marion Diner, which was located on Highway 16 South. (Courtesy of Freida Shupe.)

18

RESTAURANT ADVERTISEMENT. Since 1948, this ad for the Dixie Café and Twin Diner was carried in the billfold of Fred Williams. These two restaurants were owned by Deward Miller, who gave Fred a job as a teenager. The Twin Diner was located on Main and Commerce, and the Dixie Café was on the corner of North Main and Johnson Road. (Courtesy of Joy Williams.)

Elmer says:

"The DIXIE CAFE and TWIN DINER refuses to be undersold."

SPECIALS FOR WEDNESDAY, FEB. 27

COUNTRY HAM STEAK   -   -   - $1.00
ROAST BEEF with NATURAL GRAVY   -   .75
SALISBURY STEAK   -   -   -   -   .70
FILLET OF HADDOCK   -   -   -   .65
HOT BEEF OR PORK SANDWICH   -   -   .45

German Fried Potatoes   Whole Kernel Corn
Fresh Vegetable Salad   Green Beans
            Deviled Egg Salad

BANANA CREAM PUDDING

RESTAURANT MENU. These specials were listed on the back of the Dixie Café and Twin Diner card shown above. Business must have been very good considering the menu was dated and could be used for only the one day. Notice the prices. Today, one can hardly purchase anything for less than $1. (Courtesy of Joy Williams.)

WATER FOR MARION. Pictured here is the overflow from the Marion Town Spring. This overflow is located along the Attoway section of Highway 16 South. Since 1910, the spring has provided a continuous water supply for the town of Marion. (Courtesy Clegg Williams.)

Virginia State Fish Hatchery   Marion, Va.

MARION FISH HATCHERY. This facility on Highway 16 is the oldest of nine fish cultural stations operated by the Virginia Department of Game and Inland Fisheries. Four of these are warm water facilities, and five, including the Marion Hatchery, are cold water. Over a million trout are raised to stocking size by these cold-water stations each year. Trout are spawned, hatched, and reared here. (Courtesy Dr. Paul Brown.)

20

GRANTS DEPARTMENT STORE C. 1972. Grants was the main store in the new shopping center built on North Main two miles from downtown. Other stores included in the center were Kroger, Bassette's Restaurant, and Super-X Drug Store. Presently, Tractor Supply, Marion Family Pharmacy, Smyth County Free Clinic, Ernie Sullins Outlet, and the Pioneer Restaurant occupy spaces in this plaza. (Courtesy Gary and Bonita Frazier.)

MOUNTAIN DEW SOFT DRINK. Bill Jones experimented with soft drink flavors from 1959 to 1962 in the development of Mountain Dew. He first bottled Mountain Dew in his basement, placing the drink in old Pepsi bottles until he could not keep up with the demand. The soft drink was sold to Pepsico in 1964. In 1995, world wide sales topped $3 billion. (Courtesy Mark Byrd.)

LAKE FOREST. From 1929 to 1933, Lake Forest was a favorite with locals. This park consisted of a small lake, a bathhouse, a picnic area, and a dance pavilion. Electric lights provided illumination for nighttime swimming in the pure mountain spring water. The ruins of Lake Forest are under 20 feet of water near the center of the Hungry Mother Lake. (Courtesy Charles W. Seaver.)

Original Lake
In the new S. W. Virginia State Park, Marion, Va.

HUNGRY MOTHER STATE PARK. In 1933, John D. and Mildred Lincoln donated 1,881 acres of land to the Commonwealth of Virginia for the development of a state park. That same year, the Civilian Conservation Corps (CCC) began building roads, picnic areas, cabins, a bathhouse, hiking trails, and a restaurant. This park has also been known as Forest Lake, Lake Forest, and the Southwest Virginia State Park. (Courtesy Clegg Williams.)

DEDICATION OF HUNGRY MOTHER STATE PARK. This photo was taken on June 13, 1936, at the dedication of Hungry Mother State Park. Over 5,000 people were in attendance during this ceremony, officiated by Gov. George Peery and State Parks Director Robert Burson. This park, recently voted the number one park in Virginia, was one of five state parks constructed by the CCC. (Courtesy Kenny Sturgill.)

MYSTERY WOMAN AT HUNGRY MOTHER. This is a rare postcard of a bathing beauty at Hungry Mother State Park. Inquiries have been made as to her identity, but even Greear Studios could offer no clues. (Courtesy Dr. Paul Brown.)

CIVILIAN CONSERVATION CORPS. Pictured here is CCC Camp 1252 at Hungry Mother State Park. The CCC was a program designed to provide employment for men ages 18 to 25 years. This organization was based on the armed forces and paid approximately $25 per month. Clothing, food, and medical benefits were also provided. The CCC also had branches in Konnarock and Sugar Grove. (Courtesy Clegg Williams.)

HOTEL LINCOLN. Located between the Marion National Bank and Collins Brothers Department Store, the hotel cost $175,000 to construct and opened in 1927. There were 19 guestrooms and 13 bathrooms on each of the five floors. The hotel also included a Rexall drug store, a coffee shop, a barber shop, a beauty salon, and a ballroom. Most of the original furniture came from the Virginia-Lincoln Corporation. (Courtesy Kimberly Byrd.)

GREYSTONE MANOR C. 1927. C.C. Lincoln Sr. made a promise to his wife that if she would help him take care of his ailing mother, he would build her the finest home in Smyth County. He did just that. This English-style mansion was located at the current site of the Econo Lodge in Marion. This photo was taken after it was converted into Virginia House Restaurant. (Courtesy Kimberly Byrd.)

J.C. CAMPBELL HOUSE. This Colonial revival–style home was built around 1906 on Main Street by J.C. Campbell, the president of U.S. Spruce Lumber Company. The unusual yellow brick was shipped by rail from Pennsylvania, and the wood used in construction came from the family lumber business. Note the leaded glass sashes in the windows. (Courtesy Debra Williams.)

City View Motel, AMA Approved, Marion, Va., west end U. S. No. 11

CITY VIEW MOTEL. This motel was owned by Mr. and Mrs. George Dutton. Before the completion of Interstate 81, Highway 11 was very well traveled, and hotels and motels lined the roadside. These cozy cottage-style rooms were located on the left hand side going west out of Marion just before the highway divides. These are now apartments. (Courtesy Dr. Paul Brown.)

RAINBOW INN. This beautiful home was located on Main Street and was at one time the Rainbow Inn. Notice the stone wall in front of the house, very much like the one along the courthouse square. Observe the ornate spindles along the third-story windows. In 1932, this house was torn down to make way for the Marion Post Office. (Courtesy Kenny Sturgill.)

FORMER SITE OF GOODWOOD. Marion Middle School, formerly Marion High School, was built on the site of Goodwood, home of Arthur Campbell, in 1938. A noted Indian fighter, Campbell was one of the most influential leaders to reside on the frontier. The Campbell family was the first to build in Royal Oak, which is now Marion. (Courtesy Charles W. Seaver.)

SHEFFEY LOOM HOUSE. This small structure located at 123 Lee Street originally sat behind the James White Sheffey home on Main Street. It once contained instruments used to spin and weave cloth. Ellen Fairman Preston Sheffey oversaw the operations here and may have run the spinning wheel and loom. This antebellum building now serves as a rental house. (Courtesy Debra Williams.)

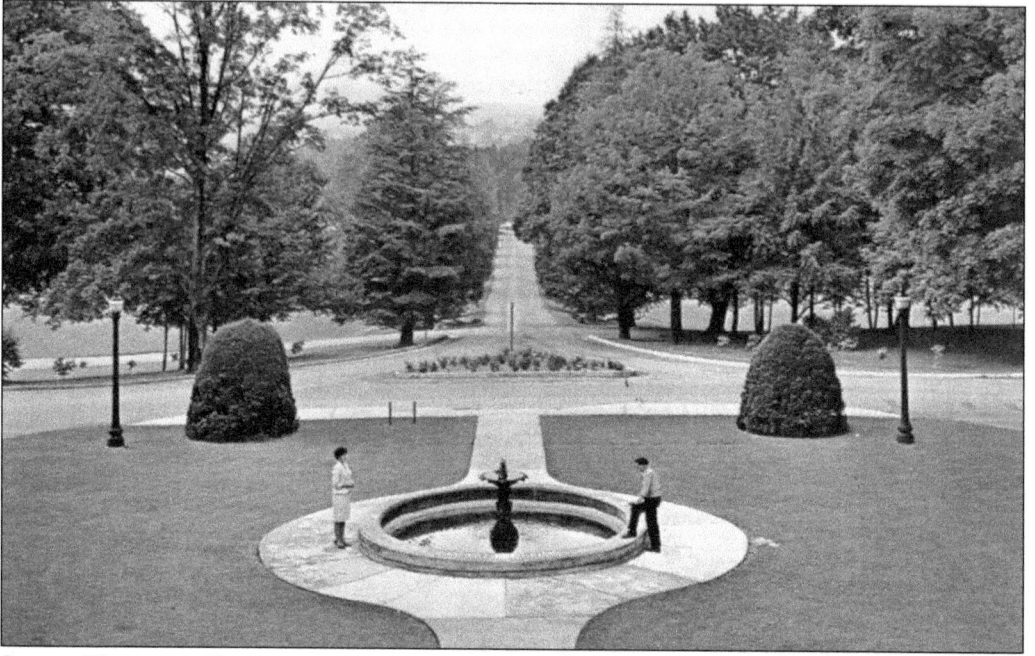

STATE HOSPITAL ENTRANCE. Years ago, this water fountain was located in front of the Henderson Building of the old state hospital. The long entranceway was lined with trees, and a flower garden separated the one-way street. The hospital has been renovated and the name changed to Southwestern Virginia Mental Health Institute. (Courtesy Edna Hutton.)

SOUTHWEST LUNATIC ASYLUM C. 1887. Prior to the 1980s, those with emotional, mental, or physical problems that society was unable to deal with were sent to institutions. Many patients lived out their lives here. During the 1960s, the hospital had nearly 1,500 patients and over 500 employees. Today, the Southwest Virginia Mental Health Institute's mission is to aid those with problems and help them to live independently in society. (Courtesy Bethana Russell.)

SEAVER-BROWN FUNERAL SERVICE. This elegantly designed hearse was once used by Seaver-Brown Funeral Home. It is unknown if the hearse was made by the family in their furniture and wagon-making business, but this is very probable. The Seaver family entered the undertaking business in the mid-1800s because of their cabinet making skills. Malcolm Brown III carries on the local family business. (Courtesy Malcolm Brown III.)

LEE MEMORIAL HOSPITAL. This building became Marion's second public hospital in 1940. Formerly the home of Wythe Hull Sr., the structure was purchased and converted into a hospital by Dr. George Wright and Dr. A.B. Graybeal. The first hospital, Homeland, opened in 1936 and was previously owned by Dr. J.S. Staley. Both hospitals were located on South Main Street. (Courtesy of Kenny Sturgill.)

ROSEMONT. This 15-room structure was purchased by Dr. J.J. Scherer, founder of Marion College, in 1878. Later on, Laura Lu Copenhaver became instrumental in a program initiated by Virginia Farm Bureau to use up surplus wool by turning it into rugs, curtains, coverlets, and luncheon sets. Rosemont served as her office and shipping and distribution point for the items created by local artists and craftsmen. (Courtesy Dr. Paul Brown.)

THE EXCHANGE HOTEL. The three-story eastern portion of this building was erected c. 1851 as a residence and storehouse for Robert A. Davis. A general merchandising business was opened here by Davis, James Pendleton, and Edward Scott. After several other owners, J.W. Fell and Minter Jackson bought the property and joined their building on the western side in 1872. The structure then became known as the Jackson Building. (Courtesy Kenny Sturgill.)

SHERWOOD ANDERSON PRINT SHOP. While at the 1927 Smyth County Fair, Sherwood Anderson heard that the *Marion Democrat* and *Smyth County News* were for sale. He purchased both and later married Eleanor Copenhaver in 1933. Anderson died in 1941 of peritonitis, the result of accidentally swallowing a toothpick. He is buried at Marion's Round Hill Cemetery. His epitaph reads, "Life, not death, is the great adventure." (Courtesy Debra Williams.)

VALLEY HOUSE HOTEL. Built in 1835, this large hotel was once called the Continental Hotel and later, Hotel Marion. Located on the corner of Main and Church Streets, it sat diagonally from the courthouse. This building contained a ballroom, poolroom, barbershop, Burgess-McNeil Furniture, and other small businesses. It was torn down in the 1960s. Wachovia Bank is currently located at this site. (Courtesy Clegg Williams.)

A STREET SCENE. This c. mid-1950s scene shows Marion Drug Store, Home & Auto, Carrier's Restaurant, Parks-Belk, Royal Oak Apartments, and the Lincoln Hotel. Presently, Hayden's World is located in the drug store building. Trade Times is housed in the Home and Auto building, and Antiques at Willow Ridge is in the old Parks-Belk location. (Courtesy Terry Hayden.)

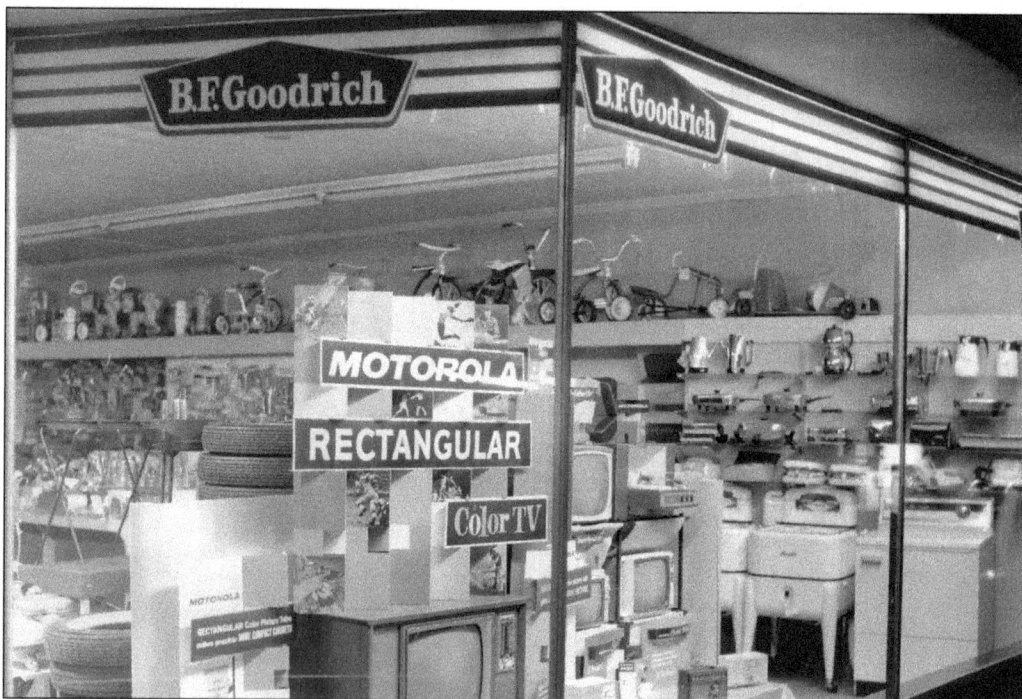

HOME AND AUTO. The Coulthard family opened Home and Auto in 1948 on Main Street. This business offered name-brand appliances, household items, hunting supplies, tires, toys, and such to the public. The Coulthards also started the first television cable system in Smyth County. This picture was taken in the mid-1960s; note the color television ad and the wringer washing machines. (Courtesy Betty Coulthard.)

32

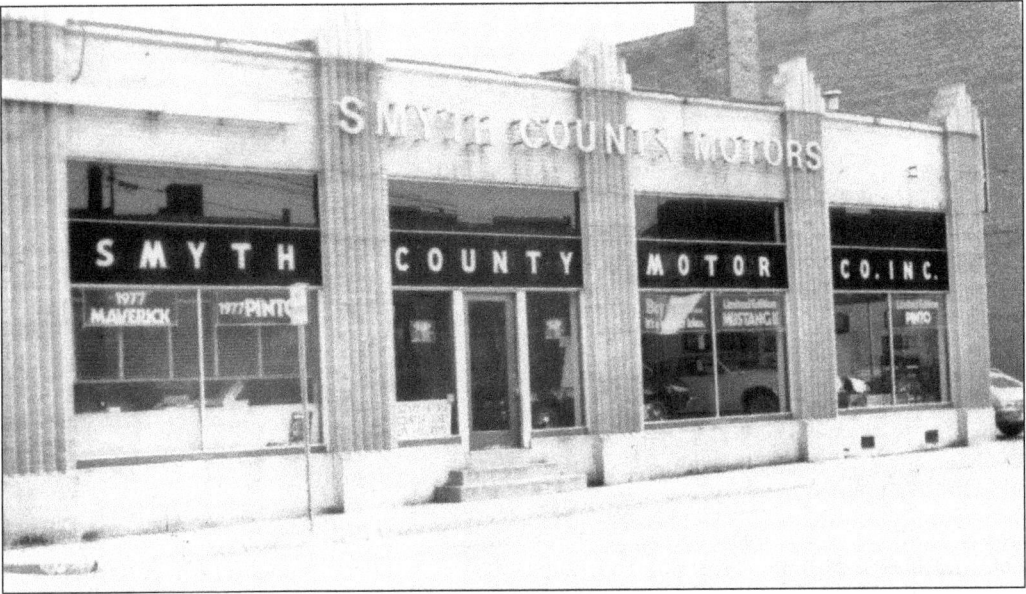

SMYTH COUNTY MOTORS. The Snider family opened the Ford Motor business on Pendleton Street c. 1927. The building was complete with a showroom for the latest models. One of the hottest-selling cars Ford produced was the 1965 Ford Mustang, which is still a collector's item. Note the signs in the window offering a 1977 Pinto and a 1977 Maverick. (Courtesy Gary and Bonita Frazier.)

MARION HARDWARE AND SUPPLY COMPANY. Organized October 20, 1900, with a capital of $4,000, the first hardware store in Marion opened at the current site of Marion Flower Shop. With B.F. Buchanan as president and C.E. Thomas as vice-president, this became the leading hardware store in Southwest Virginia. Later, it became part of the Vance Company chain. Note the clock tower on top of the building. (Courtesy Charlie Snider's family.)

D.C. CULBERT HOUSE. This was the home of D.C. Culbert, who in 1924 entered into a partnership with his brother, G.T. Culbert, and father, W.F. Culbert, forming W.F. Culbert and Sons. Their company supplied chemical limestone to the Mathieson Alkali Works in Saltville. They also provided asphaltic concrete, which was used for highways, airports, bridge floors, tennis courts, and driveways. It is located on Main Street across from Wal-Mart. (Courtesy Debra Williams.)

W.F. CULBERT AND SONS. This limestone quarry began operating in 1896. One of its biggest customers was the Mathieson Alkali Works of Saltville. Located behind the Marion Passenger Depot, this quarry manufactured lime, powdered limestone, and crushed stone. The "Rock Man," as Culbert was called, later sold out to Ellis Quarry. (Courtesy Kenny Sturgill.)

34

OVERALL FACTORY. Constructed in 1920 by C.F. Kearfoot for the North Holston Manufacturing Company, this factory was an unsuccessful venture and closed a few years later. Until proper facilities were built by the school, it was used as a gymnasium for both Marion College and Marion High School. Afterwards, it was used as a warehouse and currently houses the Smyth County Legal Aid Society. (Courtesy Debra Williams.)

THE SPRUCE LUMBER COMPANY. This band-saw mill was located on Matson Drive, at the present site of Superior Mills. The mill began operating in 1905 with J.C. Campbell as president. Later, the Spruce Lumber Company went on to start a lumber mill in Fairwood and purchased the Marion & Rye Valley Railroad. This company consolidated both lumber mills to form the United States Lumber Company. (Courtesy Kenny Sturgill.)

THE COMMUNITY STORE. This building was located at the current site of the town pool. Over the years, it housed several different grocery stores. Arthur Perry operated it at one time. Fred Williams worked for Claude Dalton and lived in the apartment above the store before moving on to work for Joe Groseclose at his market. (Courtesy Kenny Sturgill.)

GOODELL IRON FOUNDRY. G.G. Goodell came to Marion in 1859 and began operating a foundry just off Lee Street between Turkey Pen Body Shop and H&R Block. He later discovered deposits of baryta within the area and began developing it. Dr. John Apperson and Thomas W. Lumsden purchased the foundry in 1901 and reestablished it under the name Marion Foundry and Milling Company. (Courtesy Kenny Sturgill.)

H.B. STALEY COMPANY. This advertisement is for feed sold at the mill of H.B. Staley, but "Snow Flake Flour" is what made it famous. In 1905, Staley installed the first roller process in Smyth County, and his flour won the gold medal in the 1907 Jamestown Exposition. This mill was built on the Middle Fork of the Holston, where Hungate Business Services is currently located. (Courtesy Clegg Williams.)

LINCOLN THEATRE. Charles S. Wassum sold the land where the Lincoln Theatre is located to Charles C. Lincoln Sr., who built the theatre as a gift to the citizens of Southwest Virginia. The recently renovated Royal Oak Apartments are located above it. The theatre opened in 1929 at a cost of $150,000 and reopened in 2004 after a $2.1 million restoration. (Courtesy Kimberly Byrd.)

MARION HIGH SCHOOL C. 1909. This building housed all of Smyth County's students under the leadership of Clarence Campbell. This former site of the Royal Oak Presbyterian Church served as an elementary school until 1961. The Smyth County Museum and Historical Society is currently located here. (Courtesy of Gary and Bonita Frazier.)

THE BEGINNING OF AN EMPIRE. N.L. Look and C.F. Lincoln began a woodworking industry here in 1860. Their main product was farming implements. Later, a factory was built downtown and became one of the world's largest manufacturers of dining room furniture. It was destroyed by fire in 1943. The Lincolns then built a defense plant, later purchased by Brunswick Corporation and now owned by General Dynamics. (Courtesy Kenny Sturgill.)

LOOK AND LINCOLN STORE AND HEADQUARTERS C. 1900. The two-story building pictured in the center of this photo housed the company store downstairs and company headquarters upstairs. To the right of the store is the home that V.F. Lincoln built with culled plow handles. These buildings were located on the corner of Church and River Street. A dam was located just south of the factory. (Courtesy Kenny Sturgill.)

LOOK AND LINCOLN WAGON FACTORY. At the turn of the century, an employee named John Keys asked for the materials to build a wagon. He did such a good job, the decision was made to expand the factory into wagon manufacturing. Soon, they were turning out buggies, phaetons, hacks, and the like. This building was located on Church Street. Notice the houses on Chilhowie Street in the background. (Courtesy Dr. Paul Brown.)

BRUNSWICK-BALKE-COLLENDER COMPANY. Charles Jr. and John D. Lincoln inherited the Look and Lincoln Company in the 1930s. Both men developed an interest in airplanes. John D. went on to develop composites from which radomes and other plane parts are made. They bought eight acres and built a defense plant, which was sold to Brunswick Corporation in 1951. General Dynamics is currently located here. (Courtesy Dr. Paul Brown.)

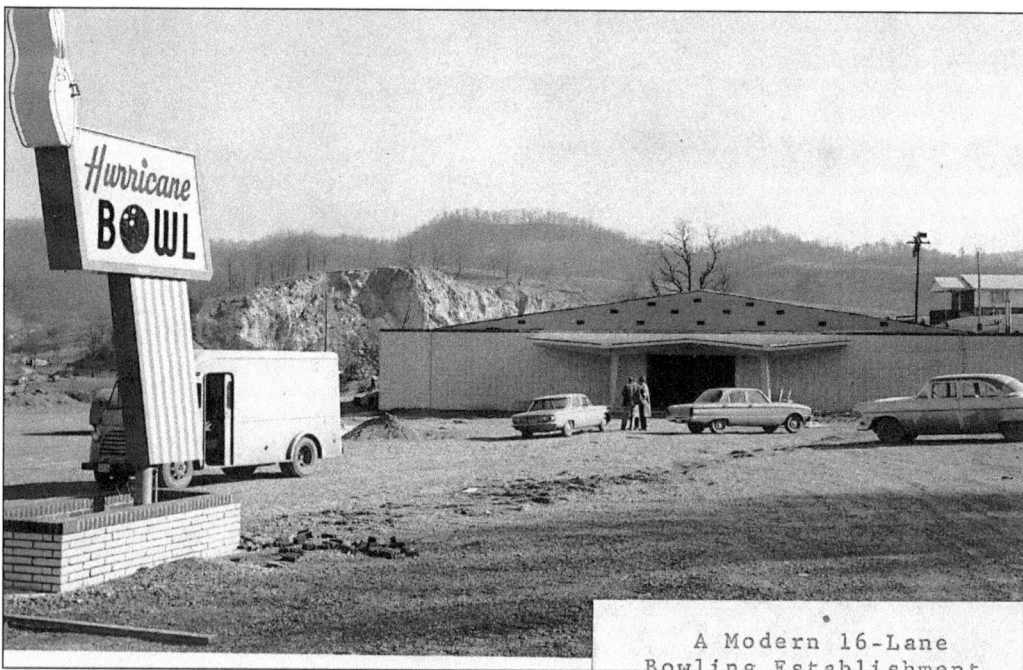

A Modern 16-Lane
Bowling Establishment

HURRICANE BOWL. During the 1960s and 1970s, employees at Brunswick were busy making bowling items and billiard tables. Property on North Main Street was rented from Deward Miller, and the 16-lane Hurricane Bowl was constructed. Bowling was a family activity. The lanes stayed busy with locals and bowling leagues working on their strikes. (Courtesy Smyth County Chamber of Commerce.)

RAILROAD CROSSING STATION. This building was once located across the street from the passenger depot on the west side of the tracks. Long cables were extended from the building to the crossing gates. When a train approached, an operator inside worked the cables by hand, extending the gates across the tracks. This structure was torn down in the 1960s, when electronic controls took its place. (Courtesy Kenny Sturgill.)

MARION PASSENGER DEPOT. Built in 1904, this beautiful structure was one of the nicest depots on the Norfolk &Western (N&W) line. It was also the only depot built in a curve on the tracks. This picture shows the water tanks that supplied the engines at the far left. The house located next to the building was the stationmaster's home. (Courtesy Dr. Paul Brown.)

MARION & RYE VALLEY RAILROAD. Chartered in 1891, this railroad was formed by Dr. J.S. Apperson and George W. Miles. Six miles of track were laid from Marion to Currin Valley to haul manganese ore. In 1896, the track was extended to Sugar Grove and a junction was formed with the Virginia Southern Railroad. Lumber, minerals, produce, farming supplies, and passengers were carried to and from Marion. (Courtesy Charlie Wassum III.)

ENGINEER'S PRIDE. This engineer poses atop his engine with pride. Because of the Marion & Rye Valley Railroad, transportation of manganese ore, iron, timber, and other products were sent to the market much faster. It was common for sparks from the engine to ignite the underbrush. Spark arresters were attached to the smokestack to alleviate this problem. (Courtesy Peggy Sexton.)

ATKINS GENERAL STORE C. 1890S. George and John Atkins started a factory at Attoway. They made hubs, spokes, wheels, tool handles, and wooden pins. Houses, churches, a general store, a post office, and a school sprang up in this thriving community. Located across from the general store, a chimney is all that remains of this factory that burned in 1928. (Courtesy Debra Williams.)

MARION BRICK PLANT. In the early 1920s, this brickyard operated two miles south of Marion. The glowing red sky could be seen for miles. Owner E.K. Coyner later sold out to E.L. Knight. The Marion & Rye Valley Railroad supplied the factory and ran alongside the kilns on its way up Brushy Mountain. Because of the plant, this community is called the Brickyard or Furnace Hill. (Courtesy Kenny Sturgill.)

THOMAS IRON WORKS. Abijah Thomas erected a 20-foot dam on Staley's Creek in 1860 to form the Thomas Iron Works. Stoneman's Raiders destroyed the iron works on December 16, 1864, to halt the production of cannon balls needed by the Confederacy. These rocks are all that remains of the once promising industry just north of the S-curve on Highway 16 South. (Courtesy Debra Williams.)

CURRIN VALLEY LUTHERAN CHURCH. Originally, this building was a one-room schoolhouse. Eventually, the children were sent to Attoway School, and Kenneth Killinger began to hold Lutheran church meetings here. This beautiful structure is still standing today. (Courtesy Debra Williams.)

44

LAUREL SPRINGS DAIRY. In 1922, G.C. Umbarger, the pioneer of modern, sanitary dairies, was the proprietor and manger of this dairy located near Adwolfe. Before dairies were established, a family cow was needed to provide milk. People milked their cows and made their own dairy products. After dairies were started, products were home-delivered. This was the practice until the late 1960s. (Courtesy Kenny Sturgill.)

EBENEZER SCHOOL. This photo was taken during the 1936–1937 school year at the Ebenezer School. The school was located beside the Ebenezer Lutheran Church and had two rooms. At the time of this photo, one room was used as a classroom and the other was the teacher's lounge. Helen Blevins Byrd is on the second row, third from the left. (Courtesy Helen Blevins Byrd.)

SKYVIEW DRIVE-IN. The Lone Star Service Station and the Skyview Drive-In were located at the intersection of Adwolfe Road and Highway 11. The Lone Star was once managed by Roy Davis, who later became Smyth County treasurer. Howard Chitwood Sr. started the drive-in c. 1948. When the interstate came through in the early 1960s, the drive-in was moved to Highway 11, where it operated into the 1980s. (Courtesy Lawrence Richardson.)

LaFAYETTE McMULLIN HOUSE. Pictured here is the home of LaFayette McMullin, one of Smyth County's most interesting political figures. McMullin served 10 years in the Virginia Senate and nearly eight years in Congress before he was appointed governor of the Washington Territory. McMullin returned to Smyth County and was elected to the Second Confederate Congress in 1863. He established *The Patriot*, a local newspaper, in 1869. (Courtesy Kenny Sturgill.)

SMYTH COUNTY'S RACE TRACK. Southwest Virginia Speedway was built across the river from Riverbend Cemetery in 1947 by Gayle Warren and John Meek. Local drivers included Smokey Bowman (car 4), Gayle and Zeke Warren, and John Hall. Gayle Warren is pictured near the track in white coveralls. Curtis Turner competed here before becoming a professional driver. (Courtesy of Greear Studios and Lawrence Richardson.)

COUNTY'S POOR FARM. This property, located on the Adwolfe Road, was purchased in 1911 from W.G. Lewis by Smyth County. The county's poor resided here and worked to pay off their debts. This was an early welfare system. In 1927, a district farm was established in Pulaski. (Courtesy Kenny Sturgill.)

OAK POINT ACADEMY. Built in 1889, this two-room school was located on the knoll behind the Adwolfe ball field. Many students and teachers boarded at nearby homes. This wooden structure was replaced by a brick building in 1915. (Courtesy Lawrence Richardson.)

ADDISON WOLFE HOUSE. Addison Wolfe was born in this c. 1828 home, and he ran a general merchandise store on his farm. Wolfe boarded scholars of nearby Oak Point Academy and charged $3.00 per month from Monday's dinner to Friday's lunch. Located a quarter-mile East of the Adwolfe Community Center, Ad Wolfe's was a popular place to shop for supplies. This community is now his namesake. (Courtesy Kenny Sturgill.)

MOUNTAIN VIEW.
Upon completion in 1857, Abijah Thomas's octagonal house and 400 acres of land were assessed at $5,000. Bricks were made by slaves within 200 yards of where the house was built. It contained 17 rooms, 10 closets, and a storage room, called the "dark room" by locals. Rumors that this room was used to punish slaves or to lock away unruly children were unfounded. (Courtesy Kenny Sturgill.)

JENNINGS'S GENERAL STORE.
In 1887, C.L. Jennings bought 417 acres in Camp and built an eight-room home and store. On their farm, the Jennings family grew fruit and vegetables; raised cattle, sheep, and chickens; and produced everything from dairy products to wool. However, the greatest thing that came from this farm was the education Jennings gave his eight children. (Courtesy Kenny Sturgill.)

MARION EXTRACT COMPANY AT TEAS. With a capacity of 300,000 gallons per day, the second largest extract plant in the world was built in the Teas community in 1910. Chestnut wood, oak, and hemlock bark were used to manufacture extract. After the lumber supply was exhausted, the plant was dismantled. (Courtesy Dr. Paul Brown.)

TEAS COMMUNITY. The Teas community was named for the president of the extract company, W.H. Teas. The houses in this photograph were owned by the company and provided for employees. Most of the men in this small community worked for the Teas Extract Plant. (Courtesy Kenny Sturgill.)

Sugar Grove CCC. Pictured here are the snow-covered barracks of the Sugar Grove CCC Camp. This government-operated program, which developed local forestlands and roadways as part of its many chores, provided employment for many young men during the Depression years. Each recruit was allowed to keep $5.00 of his small monthly pay, and the rest was sent home to his family. (Courtesy Susie Olinger.)

Hamm-Roberts Mill. In 1918, this mill was built by Famous Hamm along the South Fork of the Holston River near the Teas Community. The mill rests on the site of the old James School. A.B. Roberts bought this mill in 1922. Roberts's death in 1935 halted the mill works until his daughter, Sena Roberts Ward, restored the mill and its original machinery. (Courtesy Debra Williams.)

MT. CARMEL MILL. "Pride of Smythe" was the name given to A.F. Stone's brand of flour made at this mill at one time. The c. 1883 three-story structure was built on the site of the old Sprinkle Mill. This dilapidated building is located on Water Mill Road and is now the property of the town of Marion. (Courtesy Debra Williams.)

ATKINS ELEMENTARY AND HIGH SCHOOL. From 1906 through 1930, the Atkins School offered just one year of education for the high school students. The school held only 24 students at one time. Until a new school was built in 1930, this building also served the elementary students. Records reveal only one teacher for this school during its years of operation. (Courtesy Kenny Sturgill.)

ATKINS DEPOT. This railroad depot was located on the north side of the tracks near the Virginia House Furniture Company. Produce of many kinds was grown locally, but cabbage appears to be the biggest crop, as Atkins was once called the "Cabbage Capitol of the Southwest." Livestock and produce were hauled to and from this depot by rail. (Courtesy Dr. Paul Brown.)

ATKINS TANK. The Atkins community was once called "Atkins Tank" after Thomas Atkins, who owned the dam that supplied the water to these tanks. The steam-operated trains retrieved their water from them. Note the pens in the background, which held livestock waiting for transportation. Later, the postal service dropped "Tank" from the community's name, and it has been called Atkins ever since. (Courtesy Kenny Sturgill.)

VIEW OF GROSECLOSE. The building on the far right was once the Groseclose School but has since been converted into apartments. The service station in the right foreground was operated by Mr. Bales, who also rented out the little tourist cottages in the left front. Some of the cottages have been torn down and the gas pumps have been removed, but not much else has changed. (Courtesy Clegg Williams.)

GAMMON FARM. This newly restored, two-story brick home is located on the original "Davis Fancy" tract along Highway 11 near Groseclose. It is believed that this house was constructed around the original log cabin built by James Davis in the late 1700s as the Snavely Tavern, where stagecoaches stopped when coming though the area. It later became known as the Gammon House. (Courtesy Debra Williams.)

54

Two

Chilhowie and Surrounding Communities

Early frontiersmen envisioned a bustling town in this area and built a four-room log stockade named Town House. This fort, which offered protection against Indian raids, was later expanded to become a stagecoach inn and post office. Town House served as a meeting place for soldiers in the Revolution, the War of 1812, and the Civil War, and it was the beginning of present day Chilhowie. With the completion of the railroad in 1856, Town House was renamed Greever's Switch after the first depot agent, Bob Greever. Around 1889, George W. Palmer changed the name to Chilhowie, a Cherokee word meaning "valley of many deer." Many industries have been successful in the Chilhowie area. A pottery plant was established in 1879 by Minter Jackson. The Chilhowie Lumber Company, owned by James D. Tate and James Greever, provided lumber to the Panama Canal. Apples grown by Bonham Brothers made Chilhowie the center of Southwest Virginia apple production for years. This heritage continues through the annual Chilhowie Apple Festival. The Chilhowie Historic District is listed on the Virginia Landmarks Register and National Register of Historic Places. Tourists enjoy the scenic drive through Chilhowie and surrounding communities en route to Mount Rogers.

TOWN HOUSE. The original Town House was a log structure built on a hillside overlooking the Middle Fork of the Holston River. It served as a fort, tavern, stagecoach stop, and residence and was the start of a new town by the same name. All that remains are two chimneys located behind Food City. (Courtesy Museum of the Middle Appalachians.)

CHILHOWIE APPLE FESTIVAL. The first Chilhowie Apple Festival occurred on October 23, 1953, on the grounds of the old Chilhowie High School. An estimated 10,000 people watched the first parade, which continues to draw large crowds to this day. Other events include apple-butter making, craft and food venders, beauty pageants, and band competitions. Pictured is an old fire truck traveling the parade route. (Courtesy Debra Williams.)

H.L. BONHAM HOUSE. This Colonial-revival house is located just off of Interstate 81 at exit 35 on Whitetop Road. It was built in 1911 by H.L. Bonham, renowned farmer and owner of Bonham's Apple Orchard. The home was recently donated to the town by Bonham's children and will be used to house the Chilhowie Visitors Center. (Courtesy Debra Williams.)

JOHN S. APPERSON HOUSE. This gorgeous neoclassical-revival home was built in 1869 on 20 acres acquired from the Beattie family by Dr. John S. Apperson. He served as a surgeon in Stonewall Jackson's brigade during the Civil War. Afterwards, he returned to Town House to practice medicine. He was a founder of the Marion & Rye Valley Railroad and the Marion Foundry and Machine Works. (Courtesy Debra Williams.)

JAMES D. TATE HOUSE. Chilhowie's first mayor, James D. Tate, built this Colonial-revival house around 1902. This home was one of the first in Chilhowie to have electricity, because Mr. Tate was the operator of the Chilhowie Light and Power Company. This beautiful structure has served as a funeral home for many years and is now owned and operated by Bradley-Finney Funeral Chapel. (Courtesy Debra Williams.)

TOWN HOUSE GRILL. J.S. Morris Furniture and Henniger's Grocery originally faced the railroad tracks but were rebuilt after a fire to face the new Main Street. This building was constructed around 1910 and is now occupied by the Town House Grill and the Gathering Room, a place of fine dining, which is owned by Tom and Kyra Bishop. (Courtesy Debra Williams.)

HOTEL POOLE. In the late 1940s, the Hotel Poole was constructed on the heavily traveled Highway 11, as Interstate 81 had not yet been built. Owned by J.B. Poole, this was a very popular hotel in its time. In the 1960s, this building was converted into a nursing home. Today, Valley Health Care Center has expanded into a 207-bed immediate, assisted, and skilled nursing facility. (Courtesy Clegg Williams.)

CHILHOWIE METHODIST CHURCH. Construction began in 1893 on the Chilhowie Methodist Church, located on Old Stage Road. In the early 1800s, the first Methodist meeting house, a log structure, was built on land donated by James Thompson. On June 26, 1994, the church celebrated 100 years of ministry in this chapel with a special worship service. (Courtesy Dr. Paul Brown.)

CHILHOWIE DEPOT. Originally, the railroad installed a train car at Town House for use as a temporary depot. The town was named Greever's Switch after Bob Greever, the first station agent. Later, the name was changed to Chilhowie. The depot was located on the current parking lot of the Smyth Farm Bureau. (Courtesy Museum of the Middle Appalachians.)

CHILHOWIE'S BURNED OUT BLOCK. This beautiful architectural detail can no longer be viewed in Chilhowie because the entire block was destroyed by fire in 1904. The last building in this row was W.H. Copenhaver's Hardware Store. Other buildings include J.S. Morris Furniture, Chilhowie Tiger Brand Overall Factory, Henniger's Grocery, and Sander's Drug Store. These stores faced the railroad until rebuilt to face the new Main Street. (Courtesy Clegg Williams.)

SANDERS HOUSE. James Sanders leased the King Salt Works from Col. James White c. 1820 under the agreement that White would purchase the salt Sanders produced at a price of $1 per bushel. Sanders improved the saltworks, increased production, and threatened to flood the market and bankrupt White. As payoff, Sanders accepted this acreage, releasing White from the lease. He then built this lovely home. (Courtesy of Debra Williams.)

60

VANCE COMPANY ADVERTISEMENT. This ad, believed to have been in circulation during World War I, was a way of introducing this area to the newly formed Chilhowie Branch of the Red Cross. James D. Tate, whose wife was instrumental in starting this first Smyth County chapter, was on the board of directors for the Vance Company. Berry Home Center is located in the old Vance building. (Courtesy Clegg Williams.)

CARNER HOUSE HOTEL. This is a rare photo of the Norfolk & Western Depot in Chilhowie with the Carner House Hotel and Clothing Store, built after 1895. The hotel was torn down around 1930 to make room for the first building of the Smyth Farm Bureau. (Courtesy Dr. Paul Brown.)

WILLIAMS FUNERAL HOME. J. Aker Williams operated a furniture store and funeral parlor on Main Street in the early 1900s before building this funeral home on Church Street. The chapel was added to the building later. The Williams Funeral Home is still in business and remains in the original family. (Courtesy Kimberly Byrd.)

CHILHOWIE THEATRE AND SKATING RINK. This building once provided entertainment for the youth of Chilhowie and surrounding areas. The theatre, the first occupant of this building, charged a 10¢ admission fee. During the Christmas season, one could bring canned fruits or vegetables for admission. Later, the skating rink was a favorite gathering place. This building currently houses Superior Mills. (Courtesy Kimberly Byrd.)

HARD DAY'S WORK. J.E. Sapp leased two acres on the South Fork of the Holston River and raised tobacco on a trial basis, which he sold for 15¢ a pound. Because tobacco requires so much attention during the growing, cutting, and grading process, this product is labor-intensive. This lad, Arbin Mann, appears to be putting in a hard day's work. (Courtesy Mary Blevins.)

FIRST MISSIONARY BAPTIST CHURCH. In 1900, this church was built along the south side of the railroad by Rev. George Washington Lomans. In 1916, Reverend Lomans constructed another church, located closer to his home, installing the original bell from this church building into the new one. Lomans, a well-respected and successful businessman, owned a local store and was a schoolteacher in Chilhowie. (Courtesy of Lillian P. Thompson.)

*Town House Hosiery Plant
Chilhowie, Va.*

VIRGINIA'S BRICK FACTORY. In 1890, George W. Palmer started the Virginia Paving and Sewer Pipe Company in Chilhowie. The clay was gathered from the site of the current Little League field and land further west. This factory closed in 1910, when the clay deposits were depleted. This location has also been the home of Town House Hosiery and Buster Brown, and it is now Berry's Truss Shop. (Courtesy Dr. Paul Brown.)

Chilhowie Milling Company's Roller Mills. Chilhowie. Va.

CHILHOWIE MILLING COMPANY. Maj. Michael Tate came to Greever's Switch after the Civil War, and in 1882, he built this mill. Upon his death, his son, James D. Tate, inherited this business, which used steam for operation until electricity made its way to the area. Before burning to the ground in 1993, the mill was the oldest chartered corporation in Smyth County. (Courtesy Dr. Paul Brown.)

E.J. RUTLAND HOUSE. George W. Palmer hired E.J. Rutland to supervise his brick plant in Chilhowie. Rutland came from England in 1890, and in 1892, he built this home of ash lumber on Old Stage Road. This house was built overlooking the company's clay pits and has been kept in the family since its construction. (Courtesy Debra Williams.)

OLD CHILHOWIE HIGH SCHOOL. Built *c.* 1930, the Chilhowie High School was designed to hold 120 students. After the new high school was built in 1958, this building became the Chilhowie Middle School. Due to relocation of the Middle School, this building was abandoned for many years. It is now the home of the Chilhowie Library. (Courtesy Kimberly Byrd.)

PLUMMER HOUSE. This house was built in 1906 by "Uncle Bill" Plummer. His son, Harry, grew up here. Both were mechanical geniuses. Uncle Bill made a bicycle with wings, which went airborne on Beattie Hill. Harry, a chemist at Greever's Drug, built a working automobile out of scrap metal that the DMV registered as "Plummer's Jet." He also designed a special mixer for Greever's hand lotion. (Courtesy of Kimberly Byrd.)

SEVEN MILE FORD DEPOT. The property for the Seven Mile Ford Depot was donated to the railroad by John Preston when the railroad agreed that trains would stop here on demand or to deliver passengers. A hook next to the depot held a mailbag to be retrieved by the passing train. The post office was located just across the railroad tracks. (Courtesy Clegg Williams.)

ASPENVALE. Charles Campbell's widow Margaret and their five children moved to Seven Mile Ford after his death. She built a beautiful home called Aspenvale that has since been torn down. Charles Preston, Margaret's great-grandson, built this house overlooking the original Aspenvale site. He later sold this estate, which has since fallen into a state of disrepair. (Courtesy Kenny Sturgill.)

ASPENVALE CEMETERY. The Campbell-Preston Cemetery is located on the original Campbell tract of land in Seven Mile Ford. The graveyard has been declared a Virginia State Landmark and is also listed in the National Register of Historic Places. Inside these stone walls, which were built by slaves, lie the remains of Revolutionary War hero Brig. Gen. William Campbell and his wife, Elizabeth Henry Campbell Russell. (Courtesy Debra Williams.)

HOLSTON MILLS. The Holston Woolen Mill was located on the South Fork River about three miles west of Thomas Bridge. It was built around 1860 by Abijah Thomas, Smyth County's earliest and foremost industrialist. It was a large operation, and a thriving community called Holston Mills developed around it. The mill was powered by the large water wheel on the right. (Courtesy Kenny Sturgill.)

HUGHES MILL DAM. Just east of the Riverside Bridge, the Hughes Mill Dam is located on the South Fork of the Holston River. This dam generated power for operation of the Hughes Mill, owned by W.E. Hughes Sr. A gauging station is still located along the river to measure the flow of the current. This section of the river is a favorite spot of local fisherman. (Courtesy Mary Blevins.)

RIVERSIDE SCHOOL. The Riverside school was organized as a private high school in 1896 but was converted to a public school around 1906. In 1926, it became a junior high, and later, an elementary school. Four rooms were added in 1903 and two more in 1924. The cafeteria was built in the 1960s. The building is currently used as a community center. (Courtesy Debbie Williams.)

LAUREL VALLEY COMMUNITY CHURCH. Dedicated in 1945, Laurel Valley Community Church was built of logs donated by the Forest Service. These logs were cut entirely by community volunteers, a reflection of the commitment and cooperation of the community it served. Couples have traveled from near and far to say their vows at this lovely community chapel located in Konnarock. (Courtesy of Dr. Paul Brown.)

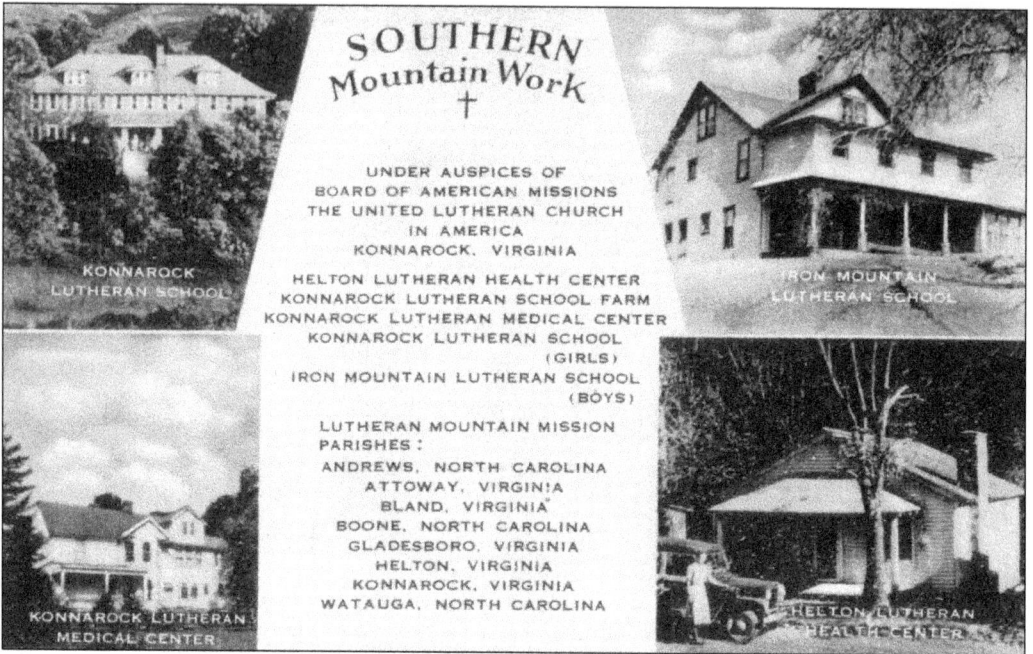

SOUTHERN
Mountain Work
✝

UNDER AUSPICES OF
BOARD OF AMERICAN MISSIONS
THE UNITED LUTHERAN CHURCH
IN AMERICA
KONNAROCK, VIRGINIA

HELTON LUTHERAN HEALTH CENTER
KONNAROCK LUTHERAN SCHOOL FARM
KONNAROCK LUTHERAN MEDICAL CENTER
KONNAROCK LUTHERAN SCHOOL
(GIRLS)
IRON MOUNTAIN LUTHERAN SCHOOL
(BOYS)

LUTHERAN MOUNTAIN MISSION
PARISHES :
ANDREWS, NORTH CAROLINA
ATTOWAY, VIRGINIA
BLAND, VIRGINIA
BOONE, NORTH CAROLINA
GLADESBORO, VIRGINIA
HELTON, VIRGINIA
KONNAROCK, VIRGINIA
WATAUGA, NORTH CAROLINA

SOUTHERN IRON MOUNTAIN WORK. Pictured here is a postcard advertising the Lutheran Synod's work in Konnarock and Iron Mountain. After the Konnarock Training School for girls was well established, the synod purchased the 33-room hotel pictured here for use as the Iron Mountain Lutheran School for Boys. Free medical services were provided to the community, and students received free religious, academic, and vocational training. (Courtesy Dr. Paul Brown.)

KONNAROCK TRAINING SCHOOL MOTHERS' CLUB. Nurse Ida Twedten arrived in Konnarock in 1928 to serve at the Konnarock Training School. She began to organize mothers' clubs to improve the health of local children. Annual dental, tuberculosis, tonsil, and child welfare clinics began. Medical treatment, dental work, and eyeglasses were provided for those in need. (Courtesy Kenny Sturgill.)

70

Home of J. H. Hassinger and Pavilion, Konnarock, Va.

J.H. HASSINGER PAVILION. After the Hassinger Lumber Company began operations, Konnarock became a thriving community. A large boarding house constructed on a site known as Big Hill, along with company homes, provided housing for employees and their families. The company also staffed doctors to provide medical care for employees. This pavilion is used for social gatherings and is J.H. Hassinger's gift to the community. (Courtesy Dr. Paul Brown.)

HASSINGER LUMBER CO. Luther Hassinger arrived in Konnarock in 1906 and built a band mill near White Top Mountain. With 300 employees, the mill processed 75,000 board feet of lumber daily. The mill sold a total of 375 million board feet of lumber during its 22 years of operation. Due to a timber shortage, the mill closed on Christmas Eve, 1928. (Courtesy Dr. Paul Brown.)

MOUNT ROGERS. At 5,729 feet, Mount Rogers is the highest peak in Virginia. It is named for Dr. William Barton Rogers, Virginia's first state geologist. Wild ponies are said to roam this mountain, where rhododendrons, red spruce, and balsam firs grow. On a clear day, one can see for miles. Many hiking trails and fishing streams encompass this mountain, enhancing its beauty. (Courtesy Kenny Sturgill.)

WHITETOP MOUNTAIN. At a height of 5,520 feet, Whitetop Mountain is the second highest peak in Virginia. Standing on top of this "bald" mountain on a clear day, one can see the states of North Carolina and Tennessee in one direction and Kentucky and West Virginia in another, all while standing in Virginia. Whitetop is well-known for its famous rock cliff, called Lover's Leap. (Courtesy Dr. Paul Brown.)

Three

SALTVILLE AND SURROUNDING COMMUNITIES

The Saltville Valley was surveyed in 1748 and granted to Charles Campbell in the name of King George II of England in 1753. The town was incorporated in 1896. Col. Arthur Campbell gave "bones of an uncommon size" he found to Thomas Jefferson in 1782. Archeological evidence suggests human occupation of Saltville for some 14,000 years. In 1980, the most complete musk-ox skeleton ever found in North America outside of Alaska was discovered in Saltville. When the Virginia & Tennessee Railroad came to town in 1856 Saltville began to grow rapidly. Two battles were fought here because of the salt, and today, the hills above the Saltville Valley still hold the earthen forts and trenches used to defend the saltworks. On October 2, 1864, Gen. Stephen Burbridge and his Union troops were defeated. On December 21, 1864, Union troops under the command of Gen. George Stoneman returned and destroyed the saltworks. However, the saltworks were up and running again in just a few weeks. In 1972, Olin Corporation, Saltville's largest employer, closed its operations, and an estimated 70 percent of the town's adults found themselves unemployed. The old slogan "Serving America with the salt of the earth" applies in more ways than one; the people of Saltville truly are "the salt of the earth."

SALTVILLE FIRE DEPARTMENT ENGINE NO. 1. This photo of Mathieson Alkali Works (M.A.W.) employees was taken in November 1926 in front of the Mathieson Office Building. (Courtesy Museum of the Middle Appalachians.)

MAIN STREET, SALTVILLE, VA.

EARLY MAIN STREET C. 1920S. This is an early photo of Saltville's Main Street. The Madame Russell Memorial Methodist Church spire can be seen in the distance. West Main Street today bears a striking resemblance to this postcard. (Courtesy Dr. Paul Brown.)

Salt Wells, Saltville, Va.

SALT WELLS. The Mathieson plant required such an enormous supply of salt that 24 low-pressure wells working continuously could not keep up with the demand in the late 1920s. Saltville's brine is very potent and contains two and a half pounds of salt per gallon, while seawater yields only one half pound of salt per gallon. (Courtesy Dr. Paul Brown.)

WALKING BEAM PUMP

WALKING BEAM PUMP. The M.A.W. began using walking beam pumps like this one, which can be seen at the Sanders Salt Park on the Smyth and Washington County line. In 1832, this boundary line was drawn through the center of old Saltville so that both counties could share in tax revenues from the salt and gypsum industries. (Courtesy Dr. Paul Brown.)

TRAMWAY AND HILLTOP, SALTVILLE, VA.

AERIAL TRAMWAY. In 1902, the M.A.W. constructed this aerial bucket line to haul limestone from the quarries, which were approximately six miles away. This aerial tramway was the longest of its type in the United States. The bucket line ceased operation in 1968 when trucks began to haul the limestone. (Courtesy Clegg Williams.)

COURT STREET. The houses pictured here were built by the M.A.W. and rented to employees. These company houses were fully maintained by the M.A.W. The company sent a maintenance man out to repair even the slightest problem. (Courtesy Museum of the Middle Appalachians.)

N.P. ROW c. 1920. This row of houses was built by the M.A.W. to house the supervisors who worked in their Nitrogen Products plant. This tidy street was called "Dolly Row" by locals because the homes had the appearance of little doll houses. These pre-fabricated kit houses were shipped to this location by railroad. N.P. Row was located on what is now First Avenue. (Courtesy Clegg Williams.)

THE MATHIESON ALKALI WORKS

Nº 21314E $10.00

Saltville, Va., _____ 19 _____

Issued to _____ Check No. _____

Drawn by _____ Check Clerk _____

THE MATHIESON GENERAL STORES
NOT TRANSFERABLE
Nº 66606 A
10 CENTS
NOT GOOD IF DETACHED

THE MATHIESON GENERAL STORES
NOT TRANSFERABLE
Nº 66606 A
10 CENTS
NOT GOOD IF DETACHED

THE MATHIESON GENERAL STORES
NOT TRANSFERABLE
Nº 66606 A
10 CENTS
NOT GOOD IF DETACHED

THE MATHIESON GENERAL STORES
NOT TRANSFERABLE
Nº 66606
10 CENTS
NOT GOOD IF DETACHED

THE MATHIESON GENERAL STORES
NOT TRANSFERABLE
10

The coupons in this book are redeemable in merchandise only by the
employee to whom issued. They will not be replaced if lost. They are
not transferable and are not good when detached.
This book must be handed to the store clerk, who will detach coupons
for amount of purchase.
          MATHIESON GENERAL STORES
The unused portion of this book will be redeemed in cash on proper
pay-day by the Mathieson Alkali Works upon surrender by the employee to whom issued.
ALLISON COUPON CO., INDIANAPOLIS, IND., U. S. A.

M.A.W. COUPON BOOKS. At one time, the employees at the M.A.W. could draw scrip in advance of wages. This early form of credit was redeemable only at the company store. The H.P. King Company in Bristol sued the M.A.W. when they refused to redeem $800 in scrip they had accepted from employees. Shortly after H.P. King won their lawsuit, the M.A.W. ceased issuing scrip. (Courtesy Museum of the Middle Appalachians.)

M.A.W. COMPANY STORE. Constructed around 1894, the company store was the largest department store between Bristol and Roanoke for over 50 years. The store stocked groceries, clothing, furniture, hardware, appliances, toys, sporting goods, and pharmaceuticals. The local soda fountain was a favorite gathering place for kids after school. (Courtesy Dr. Paul Brown.)

M.A.W. COMPANY STORE AND EMERGENCY HOSPITAL. In 1925, Mathieson established a hospital and doctor's office above the Mathieson Pharmacy. The hospital provided medical care for Mathieson employees and their families. The "Accident House," established in 1895 to care for injured employees, was located between British Row and the M.A.W. (Courtesy Dr. Paul Brown.)

T.K. MCKEE HOSPITAL. Named for Dr. Thomas Kinkade McKee, this hospital was built and owned by the M.A.W. This state-of-the-art, 44-bed facility, opened in 1950 with a staff of four physicians. The hospital was donated to Smyth County Community Hospital in 1967 as Olin (formerly called Mathieson) began to separate itself from the town. (Courtesy Museum of the Middle Appalachians.)

78

SALTVILLE STREET SCENE. This eastward-looking view includes the M.A.W. General Store and the Victory Theatre. The Rite Aid is currently located at the site of the M.A.W. General Store. The company gas station was located between the store and the Victory Theatre, which is across the street. (Courtesy Dr. Paul Brown.)

VICTORY THEATRE. The Saltville Amusement Company opened the Victory Theatre in 1922. A barber shop, billiard room, and bowling alley were located in the basement of this $40,000 building. The Victory Theatre, which seated approximately 500 people, replaced the Pleazu Theatre, a silent movie theatre. The Victory Theatre was replaced in 1948 by the Salt Theatre, which was constructed on Railroad Street. (Courtesy Dr. Paul Brown.)

BEN ALLISON'S STORE. Country stores like this one were a social gathering place in the community. Legend is that Ben Allison and two of his brothers delivered store items by mule team in areas where roads had not yet been built. Ben Allison is standing in the doorway in this *c.* 1900 photo. Confederate veteran John Allison stands second from the left. (Courtesy Museum of the Middle Appalachians.)

M.A.W. STEAM LOCOMOTIVE NO. 2. Olin donated two steam locomotives, No. 2 and No. 11, to the town of Saltville. Pictured here with four weary-looking railroad men is locomotive No. 2. Mathieson used these locomotives to pull freight cars loaded with products such as caustic soda, dry ice, and soda ash for over 60 years. (Courtesy Museum of the Middle Appalachians.)

MILL AT CHATHAM HILL. This mill is believed to be located on the site of the Holston Navigation Company. Flatboats, made here of split poplar trees, measured 60 to 90 feet long and up to 16 feet wide. Non-perishable food and supplies were floated down the Holston River regularly to Kingsport, Tennessee, and sometimes as far as New Orleans. (Courtesy Museum of the Middle Appalachians.)

Trestle containing 185,000 feet of lumber on S. G. Co's. R. R. between Saltville and North Holston, Va.
Edwin E. Judkins, Publisher

McCREADY TRESTLE. The McCready Trestle was constructed with 185,000 board feet of lumber. It was located on the branch of the railroad that was extended from Saltville to North Holston around 1905. Southern Gypsum Company's steam engines pulled railcars loaded with gypsum products from North Holston across the trestle and back to the depot in Saltville. (Courtesy Dr. Paul Brown.)

EAST MAIN STREET C. 1909. This view is of East Main Street looking toward downtown. The row of houses in the middle of the photo was built by the Mathieson Alkali Works. Today, Highway 107, which opened in 1965, meets East Main Street at the corner of these houses. (Courtesy Dr. Paul Brown.)

HARDY ROBERTS MEMORIAL POOL. This community swimming pool opened in 1943 and was built and maintained by the M.A.W. The pool contained saltwater for many years. It was an excellent place for beginners to learn to swim because it was impossible to sink in this pool of saltwater. (Courtesy Clegg Williams.)

HOTEL SALTVILLE. This 40-room hotel was built around 1896 by the M.A.W. After its demolition in 1968, a motel and restaurant were built on the site. (Courtesy Dr. Paul Brown.)

OLD PALMER INN, SALTVILLE, VA.

PALMER INN. Also known as the "Old Hotel," the Palmer Inn was built in 1858 by George W. Palmer. The meadow in front was used as a cricket field by the British for many years. The Palmer Inn was converted into an apartment building a few years after the Hotel Saltville went into operation. This handsome structure no longer exists. (Courtesy Clegg Williams.)

SCENES OF SALTVILLE. The top photo is of British Row, built by the M.A.W. in 1894 to house their British employees. The middle photo shows the Preston House (right) and the Charlie Palmer house (left). The third photo is of the Manning Palmer House, built by George W. Palmer for his brother, who managed the Palmer Inn. (Courtesy Dr. Paul Brown.)

PRESTON HOUSE. A cabin was built here by Thomas Madison in 1789. Francis Preston built this large home around the original cabin. George W. Palmer lived in the home at one time. This photo was taken during demolition in 1976. It is thought to have been the first frame house built in the Saltville valley. (Courtesy Elizabeth Harkleroad.)

1905 SALTVILLE SCHOOL. Built by the M.A.W. in 1905, this school was one of the first schools in the state of Virginia to gain accreditation. Due to the large amount of money poured into Saltville's school system by the M.A.W., Saltville's schools were ranked among the best in the state. This impressive three-story structure was built on West Main Street at a cost of $30,000. (Courtesy Dr. Paul Brown.)

R.B. WORTHY HIGH SCHOOL. While digging the foundation of R.B. Worthy High School, a large Woodland Indian site was discovered. Artifacts that were found here have recently been linked back to Luisa Menendez, the first recorded Virginian. Because this new information proves that the Spaniards were here as early as 1567, Saltville is "rewriting the history books." (Courtesy Dr. Paul Brown.)

ELLENDALE SCHOOL. F. Grundy Buchanan donated land in the Chatham Hill community for this school. It contained a total of four rooms, two for high school and two for elementary school. This building also had a library of 2,500 donated books. Still standing, this structure is located in the middle of a pasture and is currently used to store hay. (Courtesy Debra Williams.)

MADAME RUSSELL CABIN. A two-story log home was constructed by Madame Elizabeth Henry Campbell Russell and her second husband, William Russell, in 1788. Future president James Madison was a guest in the home in 1808. The original structure was razed in 1908 and reconstructed in 1974. Today, a replica cabin is located adjacent to the Madame Russell Memorial United Methodist Church. (Courtesy Mary F. Landrum.)

86

ST. PAUL'S EPISCOPAL CHURCH. The English population associated with the M.A.W. influenced construction of this handsome structure. The M.A.W. deeded the land for the church to its trustees, and building was completed in the fall of 1896. During the next three years, furniture and other items were added. Around 1907, a new Estey pipe organ was installed. Electric lights were not installed until 1912. (Courtesy Dr. Paul Brown.)

MADAME RUSSELL MEMORIAL UNITED METHODIST CHURCH. This late gothic-revival church was built from local sandstone and named in memory of Elizabeth Henry Campbell Russell, sister of Patrick Henry. Construction began in 1898, and the church was dedicated on June 3, 1900. Elizabeth Henry Campbell Russell (Madame Russell) played a prominent role in the area's Methodist movement. (Courtesy Clegg Williams.)

SALTVILLE ICE-AGE DIGS. In 1980, the most complete musk-ox skeleton ever found in North America outside of Alaska was discovered in Saltville. Other excavations have yielded the bones and teeth from wooly mammoths and mastodons, caribou, a giant ground sloth, and stag moose. In 1991, the only giant ground sloth footprints recorded in eastern North America were found. (Courtesy of Museum of the Middle Appalachians.)

MUSEUM OF THE MIDDLE APPALACHIANS. Located in the old Salt Theatre building, the Museum of the Middle Appalachians draws in over 1,000 visitors monthly. On display in Singleton Hall is an interactive model of the Saltville Valley and exhibits featuring geology, Woodland Indians, the Ice Age, the Civil War, and Company Town. The Saltville Exhibit Hall features several new exhibits each year. (Courtesy Museum of the Middle Appalachians.)

Four

MATHIESON ALKALI WORKS
AND THE MUCK DAM FLOOD

In 1892, seven industrious businessmen formed the Mathieson Alkali Works and chose Saltville as the site to build a plant to produce soda ash. It was an excellent location because of natural deposits of salt and limestone found there. Saltville was the first company town in Virginia, and as the company prospered, the town prospered. The M.A.W. owned almost the entire town, including 12,000 acres of land and the numerous houses rented to employees. The company also built the school, town waterworks, hospital, saltwater swimming pool, and golf course. In 1918, the U.S. government began construction of a $2 million plant to produce sodium cyanide. The plant was manned by 400 soldiers and 50 Mathieson employees. The war ended before the plant went into operation, and the government dismantled the plant in the 1920s. The hydrazine fuel that powered the rockets in the Apollo 11 moon landing in 1969 was also produced in Saltville. In August 1954, the Mathieson Chemical Corporation merged with Olin Corporation to form the Olin Mathieson Chemical Corporation, whose name was shortened to the Olin Corporation later. At its peak in 1960, Olin employed 1,500 people. Over 900 were on the payroll in 1972 when Olin announced that it would close its operations in Saltville. Today, the town is again producing and selling salt.

419A. M. A. Works, Saltville, Va.   G. P. Phipps, Publisher.

M.A.W. On July 4, 1895, the Mathieson Alkali Works (M.A.W.) plant shipped its first batch of soda ash. (Courtesy Dr. Paul Brown.)

MATHIESON ALKALI WORKS, SALTVILLE, VA.

SODA ASH PLANT. The tall wooden structure in this photo is the 15-story Distillery Building, which at the time of construction was the tallest wooden structure in America. By the time the plant closed in 1971, production of soda ash had increased to 1,000 tons per day. (Courtesy Clegg Williams.)

BUCKET LINE ROAD CREW. These unknown fellows made up the bucket line road crew. They cut paths through the mountains for installation of the M.A.W. aerial tramway. This photo was taken around 1902. (Courtesy Carolyn Holman.)

M.A.W. IN SALTVILLE. The first electro-chemical plant in America was built in Saltville. The first chlorine produced in America was manufactured here. Prior to its production in Saltville, all of the bleach and most of the alkali used in America was being imported from England. (Courtesy Dr. Paul Brown.)

BY PRODUCT PLANT, SALTVILLE, VA.

M.A.W. LABORATORY. The M.A.W. produced America's first commercially available bleaching powder. Their Eagle Thistle brand of baking soda cost 5¢ for a one-pound box. By the 1920s, the operations in Saltville had grown so much that chemicals were produced for hundreds of other uses. (Courtesy Clegg Williams.)

U. S. CHEMICAL PLANT No. 4, SALTVILLE, VA.

M.A.W. CHEMICAL PLANT NO. 4. Also known as the Government Plant or Cyanide Plant, this factory was constructed in 1918 by the U.S. government at a cost of $2 million. The War Department sent 400 soldiers to build this plant, which was used to produce the lethal chemical sodium cyanide. World War I ended before completion, and the plant was fired up to justify the cost and then dismantled. (Courtesy Clegg Williams.)

400 SOLDIERS IN SALTVILLE. The War Department dispatched members of the United States Army to Saltville in early 1918 to begin construction of a sodium cyanide plant. Due to the war, there was a great demand for this product. Saltville was the ideal site because there was an

M.A.W. DURING THE GREAT DEPRESSION. The plant ran 24 hours a day, 7 days a week until it closed in 1972. During the Great Depression, the men shared work, which meant that most worked two to three days per week so that no one would be laid off. (Courtesy Dr. Paul Brown.)

abundant supply of nitrogen available from the M.A.W. manufacturing process. Barracks were built to house the 400 soldiers sent to guard and operate the cyanide plant. (Courtesy Museum of the Middle Appalachians.)

M.A.W. ENGINE ROOM EMPLOYEES. Pictured here are some of the M.A.W. engine room employees. Some employees faced harsh working environments and some handled dangerous chemicals or substances on a daily basis. (Courtesy Carolyn Holman.)

M.A.W. AND EDUCATION. Most young men chose learning a trade at the M.A.W. instead of getting an education. When their sons became old enough to work, fathers helped them to acquire jobs with them at the M.A.W. At the time of Olin's closing, many employees did not have a high-school education. The average worker was 45 years old and made just above $3 an hour. (Courtesy Clegg Williams.)

DRY ICE PLANT. Built in 1931, Mathieson's Dry Ice Plant was the largest of its kind in the world. In 1954, their dry ice was shipped all over the U.S. in 54-ton capacity insulated railroad cars for use in cooling frozen foods during transit. When this plant closed in 1971, production was up to 250 tons of dry ice per day. (Courtesy Museum of the Middle Appalachians.)

THE HYDRAZINE PLANT. In 1961, the hydrazine plant was built in Saltville by the U.S. Air Force. Saltville's hydrazine has been used to power the Titan III-C and the Agena Space Vehicle, and it sent Apollo 11 to the moon in 1969. Owned by the Air Force and staffed by Olin, the $15 million hydrazine plant was the last of Olin's plants to close in 1972. (Courtesy Museum of the Middle Appalachians.)

POLLUTION. From opening operations, the M.A.W. created pollution, and as the years went by, the problem increased. By the 1950s, the muck dams held over two million gallons of lime sludge, some of which drained into the Holston River. During the 1960s, two 10-inch diameter pipes sent 1,400 gallons of sludge per minute into the waste ponds. (Courtesy Clegg Williams.)

STORM CLOUDS BREWING. In 1967, the Virginia Water Control Board adopted quality standards concerning pollution to Virginia's waterways. In the early 1970s, EPA standards required that released water contain less than 500ppm of salt, but Olin was releasing water into the Holston River that contained 4,000ppm. The State of Tennessee spent close to $2 million annually treating hard water problems stemming from Olin's contamination of the Holston River. (Courtesy Kenny Sturgill.)

OLIN'S CLOSING. On June 15, 1971, a formal announcement was made that the Olin Corporation would be closing their operations in Saltville. At this time, there were over 900 people on the payroll, meaning that over 70% of Saltville's employable adults faced a jobless future. The plant that had operated 24 hours a day, 7 days a week would soon cease operations. (Courtesy Kenny Sturgill.)

DEMOLITION OF OLIN. In 1968, Olin spent $2 million to upgrade the soda ash waste disposal method but was unsuccessful in halting pollution of the Holston River. They cited this as a reason for closing, along with the fact that the manufacturing process was out-dated. In this photo, not much remains of the once-magnificent factory that had been such a part of the community for so many years. (Courtesy Historical Society of Washington County.)

OLIN'S GIFTS. Olin made several gifts to the town of Saltville, including $600,000 in an attempt to offset some of the town's losses. The town also received 3,708 acres of land, Olin's computer building, the school system, the brine reservoir, and the old post office pictured here. This building currently houses the Saltville branch of the Smyth Bland Regional Library. (Courtesy Kimberly Byrd.)

CLEAN-UP COSTS. A recently interviewed member of the EPA stated that Olin Corporation has spent an estimated $98 million so far in an attempt to clean up the contamination from the M.A.W. and Olin's operations in Saltville. The Muck Dam site is the second largest superfund site in America. (Courtesy Clegg Williams.)

PALMERTOWN TRAGEDY. On Christmas Eve, 1924, all was quiet in the small community of Palmertown. At around 8 p.m., a roar was heard. A wave of muck 100 feet high and over 300 feet wide swept into the community below, carrying away everything in its path, including houses, barns, livestock, and people. Nineteen people perished in the Muck Dam Flood of 1924. (Courtesy Historical Society of Washington County.)

THE DAM. The dam itself was built to hold back lime sludge from the M.A.W. plant. Pipes pumped sludge into the 30-acre pond around the clock until the dam reached 100 feet in height. Note the M.A.W. smokestack in the distance. (Courtesy Historical Society of Washington County.)

THEORIES. There were several theories as to why the dam broke. One theory was that it was blown up by a man who was disgruntled because he was unable to obtain employment with Mathieson. The most plausible explanation is due to structural weakness of the dam itself. This photo shows the break in the dam. (Courtesy Historical Society of Washington County.)

THE ICEBERGS. Large chunks of the dam littered the landscape at daybreak the next morning. What looked to be white icebergs in a sea of buttermilk were actually large chunks of muck floating in gray sludge. In this photo, curious adventurers are climbing up to have their pictures made with the giant bergs. (Courtesy Historical Society of Washington County.)

MUCK DAM DISASTER, DEC. 24, 1924, SALTVILLE, VA.

CHINCH ROW. This row of M.A.W. houses, called Chinch Row, was located a quarter-mile above Palmertown and the site of the dam break. A huge chunk of the dam wall fell into the river, creating a back-wash of muck, which slammed into the hillside and destroyed these houses. Ed Stout and one of his children were rescued from his home here, but his wife and two other children perished. (Courtesy Clegg Williams.)

J.H. SCOTT HOUSE. Upon hearing a roar, Mr. J.H. Scott and his brother, J.C., ran to the door to look outside. A wave of muck drove Mr. Scott through the house and out into the yard, 50 feet from where he had previously been standing. His brother, who was visiting from Roanoke for the Christmas holiday, died instantly of a head injury. (Courtesy Museum of the Middle Appalachians.)

101

THE REFUSE. Seen in this sea of gray muck is a touring car buried up to the top of its wheels in sludge. Rescue workers removed batteries and headlamps from vehicles to provide light, but this vehicle proved to be useless. Scrap wood from destroyed houses and barns was also set afire to provide light. (Courtesy Historical Society of Washington County.)

TOTAL LOSS. Two well-dressed gentlemen are seen here surveying the damage to this once-valuable vehicle. At a time when not many people owned cars, this would have been a terrible loss. (Courtesy Museum of the Middle Appalachians.)

THE DEVASTATION. The muck dam flood would have been a tragedy on any night but was much more so because it happened on Christmas Eve. There was no warning to the citizens, some of whom were saved only because they were watching a movie at the theatre in Saltville. Note the large chunks of the dam and the scattered debris in this photo. (Courtesy Historical Society of Washington County.)

MATHIESON'S AID. Some victims lost everything. Mathieson came to their aid by donating furniture, clothing, and other items. They also placed $2,000 into an emergency relief fund and furnished housing for those who had no home to return to. (Courtesy Museum of the Middle Appalachians.)

103

Rescue Workers. Even though exposure to the lime caused sores and there was a fear that another wave of muck could wash them away at any minute, the rescue workers persevered. Christmas was forgotten as they waded in, searching for those missing. Exactly one month later, January 24, 1925, the last body was recovered. (Courtesy Museum of the Middle Appalachians.)

Muck Dam Site Today. A lot has changed at the site of the Muck Dam Flood since this picture was taken. What was once a desolate wasteland is now covered in a carpet of grass. The area is currently fenced in and has become a wild-life refuge, frequently visited by a bald eagle. (Courtesy Historical Society of Washington County.)

Five

FRIENDS AND NEIGHBORS

This chapter is dedicated to people who have contributed to our community. Many have helped preserve bits of history for future generations, while others have made history. Sherwood Anderson, Smyth County's most well-known author, moved to Southwest Virginia in 1925 and married Eleanor Copenhaver in 1933. A short-story writing contest is held annually in his memory. Smyth County History and Traditions, by Goodridge Wilson, is an excellent resource. Some authors producing major works pertaining to local history are Joan Tracy Armstrong, Elizabeth Lemmon Sayers, and Lewis Preston Summers. The four Smyth County cemetery volumes written by Mack and Kenny Sturgill are a tremendous help in genealogical research. Jimmy Warren, clerk of Circuit Court, has preserved our local history by amassing a collection of photographs and records of many elected officials of Smyth County. Lucy Herndon Crockett was a designer, an illustrator, and the author of nine books. In 1957, her book, The Magnificent Bastards, was made into the movie Proud and Profane, starring William Holden and Deborah Kerr. John D. Lincoln invented radomes, which have contributed greatly to building a strong military. H.L. Bonham was the first farmer in the United States to use fertilizer on pasturelands and wax paper to preserve apples during storage. These people, and many others, have contributed to make Smyth County what it is today. We hope you will enjoy reading about some of your friends and neighbors.

"THE FORD." Built by John M. Preston in 1842, The Ford remained in his family for 100 years. In 1942, the mansion was purchased by retired United States Army Col. Cary I. Crockett and passed down to his daughter, author Lucy Herndon Crockett. Pictured here is Miss Crockett gathering Easter lilies on her beautiful estate, which she renamed Herondon. (Courtesy Kimberly Byrd.)

LIBBY MARSH CAMPBELL. A local author of two books, Libby Marsh Campbell lived in the impressive yellow brick home at the corner of Main and Sheffey Streets. Published in 1965, *Swing Old Adam* is a book of poetry. *Make Me A Falcon*, published in 1974, is a tale of the mountain people of Appalachia. In this book, she tells of her experiences while living in a lumber camp in the South. (Courtesy Kenny Sturgill.)

GOODRIDGE WILSON. A former pastor of Royal Oak Presbyterian Church in Marion, Goodridge Wilson was also a local historian and author. One of his books, *Smyth County History and Traditions*, was written in commemoration of the 100th anniversary of the organization of Smyth County. This book is considered to be one of the foremost resources used in studying local history. (Courtesy Kenny Sturgill.)

LOLA POSTON. Born in a log cabin on Walker's Creek in 1896, Lola Poston painted the beautiful murals inside the Lincoln Theatre. She was paid $50 per painting by Charles C. Lincoln Sr. to complete the enormous 15-by-20-foot murals. She won a prize c. 1917 in England and was recognized as the "world's most naturally gifted artist." (Courtesy Kenny Sturgill.)

DR. C.C. HATFIELD. Cecil Curtis Hatfield was born in a log cabin in McCready's Gap in 1908. He worked at the M.A.W. to help pay for tuition to Roanoke College and the Medical College of Virginia. He established a practice in Saltville in 1936, where he served as the company physician for the M.A.W. until 1966. (Courtesy Museum of the Middle Appalachians.)

MR. AND MRS. JOHN M. PRESTON II. Pictured here in 1928 are John Montgomery Preston II (October 14, 1838–September 27, 1928) and Mary Lewis Cochran Preston (October 21, 1840–April 1932), great-grandparents of Elizabeth Harkleroad. John and Mary were married during the Civil War in Charlottesville, Virginia but came to Seven Mile Ford to raise their children in the old Preston House, "The Ford," built by John's father. (Courtesy Elizabeth Harkleroad.)

RECEPTION AT THE FORD. On September 4, 1895, Elizabeth Cummings Preston Gray and Robert Gray IV were married at the Seven Mile Ford Presbyterian Church. Elizabeth's parents were instrumental in having the church built, which was dedicated on July 4, 1880. After the

NELLY C. PRESTON (SEPTEMBER 1, 1880–JUNE 22, 1966). Author Nell Preston was the youngest of John II and Mary Preston's children. She was an active member of the United Daughters of the Confederacy and the Daughters of the American Revolution. After attending college in Farmville, Virginia, she returned home to The Ford to care for her parents. (Courtesy Elizabeth Harkleroad.)

ceremony, the wedding party moved to The Ford for the reception. There are at least 16 Smyth Countians in this photo. (Courtesy Elizabeth Harkleroad.)

WILBURN WATERS. In 1832, the famous hunter and trapper Wilburn Waters settled on Whitetop Mountain. On one winter expedition, he returned with the pelts of 42 wolves that he had killed. He was well-known for hunting dangerous game and animals considered uncatchable. Waters was famous for never losing the trail, and he was known to travel through rugged terrain for many days in pursuit of game. (Courtesy Historical Society of Washington County.)

MACK AND KENNY STURGILL. "Historical gossip" Mack Sturgill and his nephew, Kenny Sturgill, are pictured here. Mack's love of history and his research helped gain state historical landmark status for many local buildings. Mack and Kenny have written several books and co-authored four Smyth County cemetery books, which have proven useful for genealogical research. Their research has aided greatly in the writing of this book. (Courtesy Kenny Sturgill.)

BABE RUTH OF STOCK CAR RACING.
Born in Floyd County, Virginia, Curtis
Turner's greatest love was racing, which
he accomplished on the dirt track in
Smyth County. During his career, Turner
won 360 races in and out of NASCAR.
He was inducted into the International
Motorsports and the National Motorsports
Press Association Hall of Fame. *Sports
Illustrated* magazine named him the "Babe
Ruth of Stock Car Racing." (Courtesy
Lawrence Richardson.)

J.B. LITTON AND THE VIRGINIA HAYMAKERS. Although the Haymakers changed members
from time to time, Jesse (J.B.) was a constant in this band that played Saturdays on WOPI in
Bristol. They were invited to play at the Grand Ol' Opry, but along the way, they had car trouble
and arrived just as the show was closing. Lawrence Barnes and Sonny Coe were members of this
band at one time. (Courtesy Patty Dennison.)

MAY QUEEN. The May Day celebration, hosted by Marion College, began in 1917. The May Queen and her court were chosen from the students. Pictured here is the 1938 May Queen, Elizabeth Warriner, from Crue, Virginia. Miss Warriner later married Charles Wassum Jr. of Marion. (Courtesy Charles Wassum III.)

BLUE STEELE. Pete Peterson and Charles Wassum Jr., as college students at Washington and Lee, recruited big bands from areas such as Richmond and Knoxville to play in Marion. Many of these bands played at the Greer Tea Room on Main Street. Pete and Charles were in charge of advertising to draw in the crowds. (Courtesy Charles Wassum III.)

GEORGE W. PALMER. Responsible for changing Chilhowie's name from Greever's Switch, George Palmer built the Union Church and two schools in Saltville. He constructed the Palmer Inn and was Saltville's first mayor. Palmer owned 6,000 acres of land in Rich Valley and the largest herd of registered shorthorn cattle in the world. He started the brick plant, located at Chilhowie. (Courtesy Historical Society of Washington County.)

W.C. SEAVER. After serving an apprenticeship under a cabinet maker in Wytheville, W.C. Seaver came to Marion in 1843 and opened his own shop on the corner of Main and Commerce Streets. He later expanded operations into manufacturing wagons and caskets. In 1871, he served as county treasurer. The family-owned and -operated business he started continues today as Seaver Brown Funeral Service. (Courtesy Jimmy Warren.)

JAMES WHITE SHEFFEY. James W. was the son of Henry and Margaret Sheffey. He was well educated and was admitted to the bar at age 21. Sheffey married Ellen Fairmont Preston, and they had 11 children. He was a successful attorney, judge, farmer, and a member of the House of Delegates and the Constitutional Convention. (Courtesy Jimmy Warren.)

JOHN PRESTON SHEFFEY. The only son of James White Sheffey to reach adulthood, John became a lawyer and practiced with his father. After serving in the Civil War, he married Josephine Spiller. Their home was located at the current site of the Royal Oak Presbyterian Church, where they raised seven children. Sheffey became a circuit court judge in Smyth County and was a very respected man. (Courtesy Jimmy Warren.)

D.C. MILLER. After the Civil War, D.C. Miller came to Smyth County and founded the Liberty Academy in Chilhowie. He developed the county's education system and was the first superintendent of schools. As an attorney, Miller was instrumental in having the state locate the Southwest Lunatic Asylum in Marion and legally represented it. In 1880, he was elected county court judge. (Courtesy Jimmy Warren.)

JOHN D. LINCOLN. Though he looks like he belongs on the big screen, John D. Lincoln was born and raised in Smyth County. His family owned Look and Lincoln, which he and his brother Charles Jr. inherited. John, a great inventor, was the father of radome, a plastic used in warplanes. The factory that John and Charles started was later bought out by Brunswick Corporation. (Courtesy Kenny Sturgill.)

GOV. DAVID CAMPBELL. Born on August 2, 1779, and raised at Royal Oak, Campbell was the son of John and Elizabeth McDonald Campbell of Marion. As a Democrat, he ran for office and was elected governor of Virginia in 1837. He served until 1840. Governor Campbell died March 19, 1859, and is buried at Sinking Springs Cemetery in Abingdon. (Courtesy Historical Society Washington County.)

H.L. BONHAM (1866–1934). At age 21, Bonham started his own lumber business, which proved to be successful. In 1911, he planted apple trees on his land and soon owned the largest commercial orchard in Virginia. Bonham was the first farmer in the U.S. to use fertilizer on pasturelands, and he was awarded the highest honors of Master Farmer and the Certificate of Merit for his legendary farming techniques. (Courtesy Jimmy Warren.)

Lt. Gov. L. Preston Collins. Born in Marion, Collins later graduated from Washington and Lee University. After serving in World War I, he was admitted to the bar in 1922. Collins served as judge for the Juvenile and Domestic Relations Court. He was elected lieutenant governor in 1945 and was considered "one of the most skilled parliamentarians ever to preside over the Senate." Collins died in office in 1952. (Courtesy Kenny Sturgill.)

B.F. Buchanan (1859–1932). In 1887, B.F. Buchanan married Eleanor Fairman Sheffey. He was a schoolteacher, attorney, lieutenant governor of Virginia, state senator, and a Virginia delegate to the Democratic National Convention. Buchanan was considered to be one of the most devoted, cherished, and distinguished public servants, and he served his county, state, country, and fellow man honestly and unselfishly. (Courtesy Jimmy Warren.)

RUTH TAYLOR ALBERT. The first woman to be elected into a constitutional office within Smyth County, Ruth Albert served the community as county treasurer from 1982 to 1999. Frequently, Mrs. Albert ran unopposed due to her high popularity. She and her husband, Robert, have two children and five grandchildren. (Courtesy Jimmy Warren.)

JIMMY WARREN. Elected in 1974 as clerk of Circuit Court, Jimmy Warren is active in many organizations here and abroad. Mr. Warren is a true friend to all and is adored by all those whom he serves. He and his first wife, the late Nancy Heldreth, have three children and two grandchildren. He is now married to Charlotte Dutton. Pictured with him are some of his deputy clerks. (Courtesy Smyth County Court.)

Six

VETERANS
Defenders of Our Freedom

The Continental Congress created the army on June 14, 1775, from both the minutemen and colonial militias to defend against the British troops. These first troops, commanded by Gen. George Washington, helped to guarantee the very freedom we enjoy today. Congress formed the navy in October 1775, utilizing two armed ships to guard the coastline. The marines were established on November 10, 1775, under the department of the navy to help defend the coast. After World War II, the air force was created from the U.S. Army Air Services. Men and women have served this country since its beginning. Before they were permitted to serve, many women dressed up as men, took their firearms, and fought side by side with other soldiers. Soldiers from all religious, ethnic, social, and economic backgrounds have come together to work for the good of all Americans. They ensure the safety of our country and the rights of all. These soldiers have stepped forward, leaving behind ordinary lives and families and sometimes paying the ultimate price. We dedicate this chapter to those who have given and those who continue to give to our county.

CONFEDERATE REUNION. This gathering of soldiers from the Gibson-McCready Camp 65 occurred on October 5, 1889, which was a time to remember those who had given their lives for their cause. (Courtesy Museum of the Middle Appalachians.)

WORLD WAR I VETERANS. World War I veterans donned their retired uniforms and were guests of honor during the dedication of this Confederate cannon. The cannon was placed at the entrance of the Elizabeth Cemetery in Saltville by the United Daughters of the Confederacy. (Courtesy Museum of the Middle Appalachians.)

ISAAC MCCOY "BUD" THOMPSON, WORLD WAR II (1920–1983). Bud Thompson, a veteran of World War II, was a native of Saltville and lived in the Lick Skillet area for many years. He and Gladys Cardwell Thompson had three children—Barbara Thompson Roe, Phyllis Thompson Barr, and Robert "Allen" Thompson. (Courtesy Phyllis Thompson Barr.)

120

WILLIAM FALKE, KOREAN WAR. Veteran William "Bill" Falke of Marion is seen posing in front of army headquarters during his tour in Korea. He is married to Helen Trail, and they have a daughter, Terry Falke Foley. (Courtesy William "Bill" Falke.)

RALPH MILLSAPS, VIETNAM WAR. Veteran Ralph Millsaps, squad leader E-5 of Chilhowie, served in Vietnam. While on leave from the army, he posed for this photo with his grandmother Rebecca Weaver. Millsaps is married to Judy Heffinger and has four children and four grandchildren. (Courtesy Judy Millsaps.)

121

MARK CAUDILL, DESERT STORM. Army Sgt. Mark Caudill of Chilhowie was deployed for Desert Storm in 1991. He is married to Carolyn Millsaps, and they have two girls, Sarah and Haley. Caudill is the son of Virginia Tuell Caudill and the late World War II veteran Billy James Caudill. He is currently enlisted in the Tennessee Army National Guard. (Courtesy Carolyn Caudill.)

BRIAN MILLSAPS, ACTIVE MILITARY. Ssgt. Andrew "Brian" Millsaps of Chilhowie enlisted in the U.S. Air Force in 1998. His tours include Kuwait and Korea. Millsaps is a 1997 graduate of Chilhowie High School and attended Virginia Intermont College before joining the air force to continue his education. (Courtesy Debra Williams.)

BRIG. GEN. WILLIAM CAMPBELL (1745–1781). Pictured here is William Campbell's look-alike grandson, Francis Preston. Campbell married Elizabeth Henry, sister of Patrick Henry, and was a noted Indian and Tory fighter. As the American commander at the Battle of Kings Mountain, he turned the tide of the Revolutionary War. Brig. Gen. William Campbell is one of Smyth County's most famous historical figures. (Courtesy Elizabeth Harkleroad.)

SOLDIERS OF SIX WARS. Aspenvale Cemetery is the resting place of soldiers from six wars: Brig. Gen. William Campbell of the French and Indian War and the Revolution; Gen. Francis Preston of the War of 1812; Maj. Henry Bowen Thompson of the Mexican-American War; J.W. Anderson, George M. Cochran, Dr. Henry Cochran, Capt. Charles Preston, Capt. John M. Preston, Edwin, Henry, Robert McGrady, and Capt. John F. Oury of the Civil War; and Robert Ray Rector of World War I. (Courtesy Debra Williams.)

REVOLUTIONARY WAR MONUMENT. This monument was placed on the courthouse lawn on July 4, 1997, by the Royal Oak Chapter of the National Society of the Daughters of the American Revolution. It stands in recognition of those from this area who served in the Revolutionary War. This conflict between the 13 British colonies and their parent country, Great Britain, resulted in the formation of the United States. (Courtesy Debra Williams.)

CONFEDERATE MONUMENT. This memorial represents the endurance, courage, and patriotic devotion of those who served from the Smyth County area in the Civil War. Virginia did not cause the war and in every honorable way tried to prevent it, but when called upon, the brave men, women, and children in this proud county stepped forward to support their sister states of the South. (Courtesy Debbie Williams.)

WORLD WAR I, WORLD WAR II, KOREA, AND VIETNAM MONUMENT. This four-sided memorial has been dedicated to those Smyth Countians who gave their lives during these four wars. Listing each casualty's name, this monument honors those who paid the ultimate price. This stone rests on the lawn of the courthouse and was sponsored by the American Legion Post 18. (Courtesy Debra Williams.)

MARION VFW POST 4667 VETERANS MEMORIAL. For veterans past, present, and future, this granite monument stands to pay tribute for their patriotic sacrifices. Because of these brave soldiers, we can enjoy the freedoms we have today. No other country in the world has the privileges Americans do, and for these liberties, as the memorial reads, "All gave some. Some gave all." (Courtesy Debra Williams.)

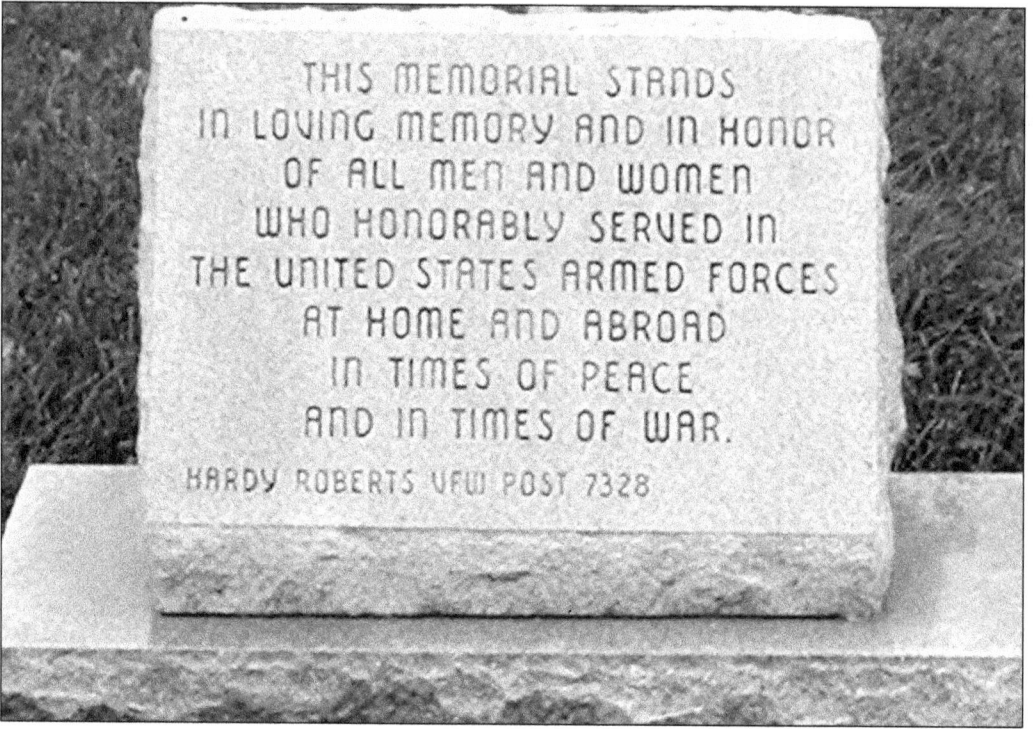

WAR MEMORIAL. This monument sits in front of the Wall of Honor in Saltville. The inscription reads, "This memorial stands in loving memory and in honor of all men and women who honorably served in the United States Armed Forces at home and abroad in times of peace and in times of war." We dedicate this chapter to all of those who have served our country. (Courtesy of Debra Williams.)

SALTVILLE'S WALL OF HONOR. Constructed by the Hardy Roberts Memorial VFW Post 7328, this memorial wall contains the names of 805 veterans from this area. Located on West Main Street, it was designed by Comrade Estil Venable and dedicated July 4, 1996. This beautiful monument is a fitting way to honor the men and women who have served our county in all branches of the armed forces. (Courtesy Debra Williams.)

HOME GUARD IN WORLD WAR II. Pictured here behind Marion High School is the Home Guard, which consisted of volunteers either too old or too young to fight in World War II. The Home Guard was a group of local men, concerned with the safety of towns where they served. This group is lining up to march in a Marion parade. (Courtesy Charles W. Seaver.)

WORLD WAR II RATION BOOK. Smyth County citizens helped in the war effort by rationing supplies in order to provide for the soldiers in the field. The 48 points in this coupon book could be used to purchase rationed items such as sugar, meat, coffee, gasoline, rubber, shoes, butter, and canned vegetables. One popular government slogan was, "Use it up, wear it out, make it do, or do without." (Courtesy Mary Blevins.)

BIBLIOGRAPHY

Allison, Roger A. *Saltville Schools, 1788–1993*. Saltville, Virginia: The Salt Center, 1993.

Armstrong, Joan Tracy. *History of Smyth County Virginia: Antebellum Years through the Civil War*. Bristol, Virginia: McFarlane Graphics, 1986.

Cole, Mattie Frazier. *A Story of the Settling and Growth of Chilhowie*. Marion: Tucker Printing, 1993.

Davidson, Ronald W. *Saltville, Virginia 1892–1998: Riding the Crest and Surviving the Wake of Twentieth-Century Industrialization in Central Appalachia*. North Manchester, Indiana: Heckman Bindery, Inc., 2003.

Eskridge, Carl V. *The Great Saltville Disaster*. Bristol, Tennessee: King Printing, 1925.

Glanville, Jim. "Conquistadors at Saltville in 1567? A Review of the Archeological and Documentary Evidence." *The Smithfield Review*. Blacksburg, Virginia: Pocahontas Press, Inc., 2004.

Kent, William B. *A History of Saltville*. Radford, Virginia: Commonwealth Press, 1955.

Layne, Thomas A. *Memories 20s, 30s, 40s*. Thomas A. Layne, 1993.

Mauck, J. Leonard. *History of Education in Smyth County*. Alexandria, Virginia: National Printing Company, 1978.

Peters, Margaret T. *A Guidebook to Virginia's Historical Markers*. Charlottesville, Virginia: The University Press of Virginia, 1985.

Presgraves, Jim. *Smyth County Families and History*. Pulaski, Virginia: B.D. Smith Printing Co., 1974.

Preston, Thomas L. *Historical Sketches and Reminiscences of an Octogenarian*. Richmond, Virginia: B.F. Johnson Publishing Co., 1900.

Sayers, Elizabeth Lemmon. *Smyth County Virginia: Pathfinders and Patriots*. Marceline, Missouri: Walsworth, 1983.

Smyth County News. Marion, Virginia: 1970–2004.

Summers, Lewis P. *History of Southwest Virginia, 1746–1786, Washington County, 1777–1879*. Baltimore: Regional Publishing Company, 1971.

Sturgill, Mack H. *Abijah Thomas and His Octagonal House*. Marion: Tucker Printing, 1990.

Sturgill, Mack H. *Hungry Mother: History and Legends*. 2nd Ed. Marion: Tucker Printing, 2001.

The Smyth County Heritage Book Committee and Don Mills, Inc. *Heritage of Smyth County Virginia 1832–1997*. Marceline, Missouri: Walsworth, 1997.

Turnage, Martha A. *Company Town Shutdown*. Annapolis: Berwick Publishing, 1994.

Wilson, Goodridge. *Smyth County History and Traditions*. Radford, Virginia: Commonwealth Press, 1932.

www.ingramcontent.com/pod-product-compliance
Lightning Source LLC
Chambersburg PA
CBHW050555110426
42813CB00008B/2362